Quest

Competitive Advantage and the Art of Leadership in the 21st Century

Dean van Leeuwen

2015 Edition

All feedback welcomed on
quest@tomorrowtodayglobal.com

All the best on your
2016 Quest

Dedication

My wife and son. For their fun and loving support.

My mother and father. For their tenacity, zest and creative spirit.

My sister. For her kindness and generosity.

Table of Contents

Prologue - The Tortoise and the Hare 8

Introduction 11

Part One - The Power of Delivering Meaningful Benefits 16

    Chapter One - The Worst Disease You Have Never Heard Of.............17

    Chapter Two - Perversions of the Proper Workings of Capitalism...31

    Chapter Three - A Generation of Questers....................................40

Part Two - The Power of Achieving the Impossible 50

    Chapter Four - The Greatest Scientific Quest of the 21st Century.....51

    Chapter Five - The Greatest Scientific Quest of the 18th Century.....61

    Chapter Six - Making The Impossible Possible 77

Part Three - The Power of a Target Destination 88

    Chapter Seven - Adventurous Journeys 89

    Chapter Eight - The Greatest Quest in Sports History 94

    Chapter Nine - Wrong Destination, Right Idea.......................106

    Chapter Ten - Right Destination, Right Idea...........................112

Final Thoughts 120

Acknowledgements 135

Sources..137

About the Author...142

About TomorrowToday Global..143

Prologue

The Tortoise and the Hare

1.

Aesop's fables tell a story of the tortoise and the hare who decide to race against each other. The hare is so confident of winning that he lies down halfway through and goes to sleep. The tortoise, knowing he must work hard to win, plods along without stopping until he passes the sleeping hare and wins.

There is an age-old adage that says: More haste, less speed. Success is the result of hard work, perseverance and dedication. This approach is favoured and rewarded across all aspects of life from education, leadership and performance management, to Wall Street and bankers, all looking for a steady track record of results. This mindset has become part of the lexicon of scientific management and translated into a single-minded drive towards increased organisational efficiency and effectiveness.

Aesop was a slave and storyteller who lived in ancient Greece between 620 and 560 BC. His fables have descended through the ages to modern times and been reinterpreted in both popular and artistic media. Over the years, various interpretations of the fable have evolved. In 1857, Charles Bennett, a Victorian illustrator and pioneering cartoonist, sketched a satirical image of *The Tortoise and the Hare.* In the image the tortoise was depicted as a smug industrialist standing outside the Guildhall, too fat and arrogant to move but holding the hare, who is depicted as a worker or entrepreneur, prostrate under his foot.

In *The True History of the Tortoise and the Hare* published under the name Lord Dunsany, prolific Irish writer and dramatist Edward

Plunkett suggests another interpretation of the fable. In his version the hare, recognising the stupidity of the challenge pulls out of the race. His abdication means that the tortoise wins by default. When interviewed what his victory signifies, the tortoise says, "It is a glorious victory for the forces of swiftness." And all his followers say "nothing else for years". According to Plunkett, the reason that this version of the race is not widely known is because "very few of those that witnessed it survived the great forest-fire that happened shortly after. It came up over the weald by night with a great wind... they hurriedly called a meeting to decide what messenger they should send to warn the beasts in the forest. They sent the Tortoise."

Until the 18th century, preachers, speechmakers and puritans mainly employed the fables. The philosopher John Locke, who was one of the most significant Enlightenment thinkers, influenced the evolution of these fables towards a younger audience. For him Aesop's fables were: "Apt to delight and entertain a child... yet afford useful reflection to a grown man. And if his memory retain them all his life after, he will not repent to find them there, amongst his manly thoughts and serious business."

It is therefore not surprising that with the onset of the Industrial Revolution vast numbers of fables were published. The masters of the Industrial Revolution approved of stories propagating hard work and perseverance within a framework of control, conformity and compliance – the 3Cs of management. *The Tortoise and the Hare* for all its sound advice was a firm favourite. Leagues of industrialists would have hard workers believing risk is a bad thing and adherence to the 3Cs would be rewarded. But what if in a changing world efficiency and effectiveness are no longer the bastions of competitive advantage? Like the backers of the tortoise who shouted: "Run hard. Run hard, hard shell and hard living: that's what has done it", are today's leaders making the same error believing efficiency and effectiveness to be the best way? What if what modern organisations need is more hare and less tortoise? As the CEO of industrial giant GE, Jeff Immelt says, "Ten or twenty years ago, what differentiated companies was how well managed they were. Today if you are well managed, you can still be a good company, but you're not going to be a dominant company."

In the following pages, I will argue that the global industry's internalised mindset of control, conformity and compliance, which focuses incessantly on efficiency, effectiveness and risk aversion now stunts growth and innovation, and acts as the greatest obstacle to success in the future. I'm not saying that organisations do not need to be effective and efficient. Of course they do. But these qualities no longer offer competitive advantage. What I am saying is that it's time to release the hare – Bennett's cartoon – or to inspire and convince the hare to engage in the challenge – Plunkett's version, whichever you prefer. In the 21st century, which has the potential to deliver so many wondrous advances, engaging people to deliver creative and disruptive innovation is going to be critical for success and gaining competitive advantage. And the best way to achieve this is through the power of the leaders' quest.

Introduction

Quests are part of every culture's folklore and their stories are as old as civilisation itself. The epic of Gilgamesh is an adventure story from ancient Mesopotamia. Homer's *Odyssey* and *King Arthur and the Knights of the Round Table* are mythical quests. Columbus's and Cook's Voyages of Discovery were quests of human endeavour as are more recent-day escapades such as the race to capture the South Pole; summiting Mount Everest; and, putting a man on the moon. Heroes go out into the unknown, endure various tests, are forced to back up, unlearn and relearn, then hopefully they return successful with a boon.

Quests are the inspiration propelling civilisations forward and this book reveals how this powerful force can be harnessed for your own future success. So each chapter tells an inspirational story of a quester – organisation or person – famous or unknown, genius or "crazy", crusader or reluctant hero, ordinary or brilliant – who had a bold idea and set off on a quest that made a meaningful difference to the lives of people around them. Questers embark on adventurous journeys that change the future. Questers by their very nature are disruptors.

People are drawn to quests, captivated by the endeavours, fascinated by the stories, motivated, inspired by their challenges and excited to be part of their successful conclusion. *National Geographic*, a publication well known for visually capturing the exploits and stories of great adventurers on quests says that the "Latin root of the word, oddly enough, means 'an arrival', but adventure almost always entails a going out, and not just any going out but a bold one. It is a quest whose outcome is unknown but whose risks are tangible, a challenge someone meets with courage, brains, and effort—and then survives, we hope, to tell the tale."

My research reveals three qualities of a quest: delivering meaningful benefits; achieving the impossible; and having a target destination. In this book these qualities are used as a framework to explore why quests have proven to be such powerful agents of change since the dawning of civilisation. *Quest* also shows how leaders can leverage the three qualities to embark on quests of their own.

Sebastian Thrun, a founder of Google X, a research laboratory at Google, says, "I believe we live in an age where most interesting inventions have not been made, where there are enormous opportunities to move society forward. I'm excited to live right now. But I would rather live 20 years from now or 50 years from now than live today. It's going to be better and better." He continues by explaining, "with the advent of digital information, the recording, storage, and dissemination of information have become practically free. The previous time there was such a significant change in the cost structure for the dissemination of information was when the book became popular. Printing was invented in the fifteenth century, became popular a few centuries later, and had a huge impact in that we were able to move cultural knowledge from the human brain into a printed form. We have the same sort of revolution happening right now, on steroids, and it is affecting every dimension of human life."

An important idea explored in this book, therefore, is that a new pioneering age of exploration and adventure has been thrust upon us. This period of disruption is the Age of Quests and it is heralding incredible pioneering journeys into all fields of space exploration, health, science, education, engineering and more. During the Age of Exploration, the Enlightenment and the Industrial Age, brave souls endeavoured to discover new lands and opportunities. Once again humanity faces an awe-inspiring era when individuals have access to emerging technology and discoveries that will reshape the world in which we live. Those open to learning and mastering the new paradigms required to be successful in this new era will be rewarded with extraordinary riches and fame.

Everything that was achieved in the past 200 years of industrialisation has the potential to be dwarfed by the technology, knowledge advances and capabilities of the 21st century. It is not inconceivable that, by the middle of this century, we will have the technology to provide for the next million years an endless supply of abundant, cheap and pollution-free energy, using a stable isotope of hydrogen found plentifully in sea water. Furthermore we might be able to eradicate major diseases like cancer, Alzheimer's and dementia and even double life expectancy to over 150 years of age. Many of the things that seemed once to be science-fiction or fantasy the first human settlement on Mars, self-driving cars, super-strong super-light materials that enable electric passenger planes are fast becoming a reality. We have the smart machines, robots, technology and, increasingly, the knowledge to achieve things that will blow us away in wonderment.

But, equally, there are immense seemingly insurmountable challenges. As Professor Ian Goldin, director of Oxford University's Martin School, a world-leading centre of pioneering research for a sustainable and inclusive future says, "This could be our best century ever – or our worst." I want Sebastian Thrun to be correct in his prediction of things getting better and better, not only for my son who will be 22 in 20 years time but also for a generation of his peers who are growing up in a world where the future looks increasingly uncertain.

The next three decades will decide the outcome of this century. Urgency is required if we are to address the challenges humanity and our world face. I believe we can find solutions if we mobilise everyday leaders to discover their quests.

Worryingly, very few companies or individuals are on quests to make meaningful and significant differences to their world. Most organisations avoid risk and meaningful change seeking only profit maximisation and incremental gains in efficiency. What I term "incrementalisation" – a strategy of incremental gains delivered through increased efficiency and effectiveness – does not mean you will fail dramatically, but you are certain not to succeed massively either. This is of deep concern as we live at a time when being creatively conservative is not a formula for constructing a future world capable of developing solutions to sustain and improve the lives of the 9.6 billion people who will inhabit our blue planet by the middle of the 21st century.

To achieve this century's awesome potential and ensure the dawning of a new great era, humanity needs leaders with the courage to embark on world-changing quests. So another idea in this book is that those people and organisations that will be most successful in the future will embark on quests to make a meaningful difference in the world. *Quest* shows that by understanding the mindset of the quester, leaders can shape competitive advantage and build a positive future for themselves, their organisations and the societies they touch.

The good, no, the great news is that the mindset of a quester is a leadership skill we can all cultivate. Contrary to popular belief, a quest is not some knightly or mystical birthright given to a fortunate few. Anyone can embark on a quest. Quests can be big or small, personal or professional. In this book, you will meet horologists, artists, venture capitalists, electrophysicists, CEOs, educators, visionaries and ordinary people, all of whom are very good at what they do, and who owe their success to their particular quest. Each story helps to identify and unpack the three qualities of a quest and gives you a model to plot your own successful questing adventure.

Quest explores what it takes to be a quester and the lessons quests bestow on organisations and leaders who want to make a powerful difference to the lives of their customers, colleagues and society. This is not a book about grand quests like going to Mars but rather about how, through the power of quest, a special breed of dedicated everyday leaders are driving the strategic agenda and changing the world around them for the better. Through their stories I hope you will be inspired to embark on your own "world-changing" adventure.

Part One

The Power of Delivering Meaningful Benefits

"Institutions will try to preserve the problem to which they are the solution."
Clay Shirky

Chapter One

The Worst Disease You Have Never Heard Of

"Everyone understands a quest."
Sarah Dessen

1.

Rafaella Lily or Rafi as her parents call her is a normal seven-year old except for one thing; *she has "the worst disease you've never heard of."* Born November 2007, a beautiful baby girl to her proud parents Jackie and Brett Kopelan, Rafi just happened to be missing skin on the back of one hand and her feet. Arriving two weeks past her due date the on-call paediatrician said, "Don't worry about it. She's just overcooked; we've seen it before," but six hours later Rafi was taken into the neonatal intensive care unit where she would spend the next 34 days. A biopsy revealed that Rafi was lacking the collagen VII protein resulting in an extremely rare condition known as dystrophic epidermolysis bullosa or EB.

In the United States one in 20,000 births or around 200 children a year are affected by this very serious genetic condition. Dr Jakub Tolar, an expert on rare skin disease explains that humans have: "Several layers in the skin, and the two main layers – the dermis and the epidermis – are literally glued together like Velcro with loops of this collagen. If you don't have collagen, you will lose the surface of the skin, and that's what these kids don't have."

With skin as delicate as butterfly wings these children are so fragile that even the slightest touch can cause a tear resulting in severe blistering. In Rafi's case, which is considered severe, just running a finger along her arm risks removing a layer of her skin. Blisters on her hands have caused her fingers to fuse together and if her parents, through a show of loving affection, cup her face in their hands and kiss her on the forehead, the skin risks being peeled off like tissue paper. As a father of a toddler I can't even begin to imagine just how awful it must be never to be able to cuddle, kiss or fling your child in the air and catch him for fear of tearing his skin. Each day, Brett and Jackie spend up to 90 minutes carefully wrapping, unwrapping and bathing every inch of Rafi in special bandages and gauze; and, even though up to 75 percent of her body can be covered in lesions Rafi endures baths with diluted vinegar or bleach. "It's hard to torture your child on a daily basis in order to keep her safe," Brett says in an interview with *Boston Magazine*, "that's really what you're doing when you're bathing her."

There are five classifications of the disease based on degree of severity. At its most severe, which Rafi has, it is an awful debilitating disease that causes ruptures both inside and outside the body. Food being eaten can tear away skin, and blisters erupt in the oesophagus making it near impossible for patients to eat anything solid. The disease also puts victims at high risk of developing skin cancer. "These children suffer terribly, then they develop a fatal cancer in their adult years," says Philip Reilly, who specialises in rare diseases. Most people with EB pass away at a young age with only a few making it into their thirties.

There is currently no effective therapy for EB and since the Great Recession, research and drug development by drug companies, federal grants and venture capital has been dramatically cut back. According to the MoneyTree Report from PricewaterhouseCoopers, approximately $780 million of venture capital went to life sciences companies in the first quarter of 2012, a breath-taking 43 percent drop. Even more disturbing is that the vast majority of that money went to existing companies with products in late-stage development, not to start-ups or new drug trials. The amount of money for first-time biotech company financing has fallen by over 60 percent.

Money that used to be available to finance life-saving therapies has disappeared. And this isn't a one-time glitch; it's a long-term trend. In 2000 there were 1,022 biotech start-ups in the industry, 10 years later the number of active firms had plummeted by over 50 percent to just 462. All of this despite amazing advances and the life-changing potential that lies behind nascent technology innovations in DNA sequencing, microRNA, drug delivery, diagnostics, and more.

The truth is for venture capital companies it has become far more lucrative and easier to back the next Uber or Instagram than to take the risk of funding a drug innovation that would change the lives of patients. When funding that could be directed to industries that advances humanities is squandered in preference for technology that hardly raises the social-development metre, then the system is failing profoundly. So it was with elated surprise that Brett Kopelan heard of a venture capital firm that had invested in a promising start-up biotech company that is developing a collagen replacement technology for the treatment of EB.

2.

"I don't think we live in an incredibly fast technological age," says Peter Thiel, the cofounder of PayPal and one of the early investors in Facebook. "We have not had meaningful technological innovations since around the 1970s." Thiel's investment fund – The Founders Fund has over a billion dollars under management. To reflect their interest in potential world-changing bold innovations, the fund's slogan takes a mischievous swipe at current innovations: "We wanted flying cars, instead we got 140 characters." Thiel insists this is not a criticism of Twitter as a business. Twitter "will eventually become profitable," he says, "but its specific success may be systematic of a general societal failure. Even though it improves our lives in certain ways, it is not enough to take our civilisation to the next level." The thing is, all the investment and focus on the Internet and mobile technology helps with improving communication and this enables us to make our lives and businesses much more efficient. However, innovations in areas of energy, transport, medical and engineering have largely only been incremental not revolutionary over the past three decades. "We are living in a material world, so that's a pretty big miss out," concludes Thiel.

Thiel is not alone in his thinking; there is a growing sentiment that Silicon Valley, the impetus driving the industrialised world, is disconnected from the realities and challenges of the 21st century. Mike Steep, the senior vice president of global business operations for Xerox's legendary innovations laboratory PARC, says, "This town used to think big – the integrated circuit, personal computers, the Internet. Are we really leveraging all that intellectual power and creativity creating Instagram and dating apps? Is this truly going to change the world?"

From Steep's office on Coyote Hill Road, he has a spectacular panoramic view of the valley stretching from Redwood City to Santa Clara. Here we find the heartbeat of the global economy and the racing pulse of many of her superstars: Hewlett-Packard, Oracle, Facebook, Google, Netflix and Intel. Driving from his PARC office for 10 minutes in a south-easterly direction on Route 280, brings you to Steve Jobs's childhood home. This is where the majority of disruptive innovations in modern history have originated and yet today from where Mike Steep stands and views the valley, he is disillusioned, "I see a community that acts like it knows where it's going, but that seems to have its head in the sand."

Robert Gordon, an economist and highly distinguished academic at the Northwestern University in the United States believes that economic growth, like that seen during the Industrial Revolution, is behind us. "I am not forecasting an end to innovation," says Gordon, "just a decline in the usefulness of future inventions in comparison with the great inventions of the past." The problem civilisation faces, Gordon argues, is that the "low-hanging [innovation] fruit has already been picked." To support his argument Gordon, who commands $20,000 for an appearance as a speaker on the US conference circuit, uses a convincing anecdote. He reveals a picture of a toilet and a smartphone and then asks the audience a brutally simple but effective question, "Which would you give up?" It's a sobering thought because as wondrous as many of the digital age innovations are, their impact is not, at least not yet, on the same level as early Industrial Revolution innovations such as electricity, household plumbing and the internal combustion engine. "There will continue to be great inventions in the future", says Gordon. "But they aren't likely to power growth the same way as, say, the advent of the automobile." Thiel agrees with Gordon, however, he argues that there has never been any low-hanging fruit, "It was always intermediate height and the question was, were people reaching for it or not." Thiel says he is, "frustrated because I think technology is progressing too slowly, but I'm optimistic because I think it could be going a lot better."

3.

It was the economist and Nobel Prize winner Robert Solow who first argued in the 1950s that growth was driven by new technology. Because economic growth is tied to innovation and if, as Thiel, Gordon and Steep, argue innovation has stagnated since the 1970s, then it stands to reason that economic growth and prosperity too will be drying up.

Here's the stark reality: the actual economic experience of the middle-class American, or European, has been rather disappointing over the past three decades. Even growth in emerging powerhouses like China and India is slowing. Perhaps the slowing global growth is not an aberration after all. Perhaps low-growth and flat-line wages are going to be the new normal in the future. Such a gloomy forecast may seem startlingly improbable, after all, every generation in living history, has recognised a doubling in lifestyle over the previous generation. However, economic figures are revealing a troubled truth. In real terms the vast bulk of the population in developed economies from the US to the Europe are no better off than they were in 1973. Over the past four decades, median real household income has actually risen by only 0.1 percent per annum.

The growing inequality gap between the top one percent and the other 99 percent has reached immoral and unsustainable levels. The top one percent of the population has over 35 percent of the accumulated wealth; the top 0.1 percent has over 15 percent. Inequality in the United States and Europe is "probably higher than in any other society at any time in the past," says French economist Thomas Piketty in his best-selling book *Capital in the 21st Century.* According to *Forbes Magazine*, a business publication, CEOs make upwards of 331 times what the average worker earns. That's not the lowest-paid employee, for example the janitor, but the average earner in his or her company. To put this into perspective, the average worker needs to work more than a month to earn what the CEO makes in one hour. At the extreme end, for example, minimum-wage employees at Walmart would have had to work 1,372 hours to earn what their then CEO, Michael Duke made in one hour in 2013. Assuming the average worker works 170 hours a month, that's eight months of slog before the minimum-wage earner matched the now ex-CEO of Walmart's hourly wage. Inequality is a growing threat to prosperity and civilisation, as we know it in the 21st century.

If the gap is not closed, inequality will continue to fuel the fire of fundamentalist bodies like the Islamic State and other revolutionary radicals who believe the current system is iniquitous and are leading a quest of their own with horrifying consequences, if successful. We live in a civilised world, but do not believe we are too civilised for history to repeat itself. Revolutions throughout history happen when the have-nots say enough is enough. It's worrying to note as Oxford University professor Ian Goldin points out, "by 2030 an individual using a biopathogen will have the ability to wreck it all."

The quest to close the inequality gap is one of our most pressing and urgent challenges and there are many others. Sadly, most of our current leaders who are found at the helm during this revolutionary

Age of Quests are focused on protecting the old world, defending old paradigms and safeguarding wealth and ways of living that are holding society and civilisation back. As in Charles Bennett's cartoon of the fat tortoise holding the hare prostrate, today's institutions and institutionalised managers are often found holding back creative ideas and talented questers. One of the challenges you will experience when embarking on a quest to deliver meaningful benefits is that you will come up against the "establishment", those who guard the old world and feel threatened by the disruptions your quest will create. Here is the snag, the conventional wisdom of management, especially the 3Cs and an incessant focus on cost reductions and chasing quarterly revenue targets, is preventing leaders and society as a whole from making major advances in important areas that could make the world a better place.

Keith Yamashita, a consultant who has worked with greats like Steve Jobs and Starbuck's CEO Howard Schultz, says they figured out the one key thing every great leader knows. "First, you must have a sense of purpose. The belief that what we are doing will make a difference in the world." The belief that what you are doing will deliver meaningful benefits to the world – be it on a global scale or at a macro level – with customers, colleagues or family – is an extremely important and powerful quality of a quest.

With all of this in mind, the encouraging news is there is a new and growing group of leaders who are inventing business models with core strategies to deliver meaningful benefits first and foremost to society and the world. In doing so they are creating sustainable competitive advantages.

4.

Tim Allen, Martin Lawrence, William Macy and John Travolta star in the movie *Wild Hogs*, a story about four suburban biker wannabes seeking adventure on the open road. Dressed from head to toe in Hell's Angels leathers these Baby Boomers – people born in the 1940s and

1950s – take on the world and win. It's the classic stereotypical tale of a generation that has transformed the world and still desires to do more. The founders of Third Rock Ventures are the real-life counterparts of the characters in *Wild Hogs*, except exchange the Hell's Angel hopefuls and Harley-Davidsons for venture capitalists changing the world of biochemistry. Their bond – a common loathing for a drug industry's focus and reputation on valuing profits over patients.

The name Third Rock does not come from the sitcom series about four aliens who settle on Earth, but from a documentary by the same name about Earth and her frailness. Operating out of an office in Boston's Newbury Street, a trendy neighbourhood filled with high-end boutiques and cafes, these revolutionaries come clad not in corporate suits and ties but wearing "Beach Punk 1982" T-shirts, camouflage shorts, funky scarves and skull-ring jewellery. Since 2007, coincidently the same year *Wild Hogs* was released, Mike Levin, Kevin Starr and Bob Tepper, the three founding partners of Third Rock Ventures, have been "company builders" and they are on a quest to: "Take bold scientific ideas and turn them into great companies with the potential to make a dramatic difference in patients' lives."

Quests involve endeavours that deliver meaningful benefits to the world. Like the Wild Hogs in the movie, Levin, Starr and Tepper sought an adventure, but one where they could contribute to making a meaningful difference. Their adventure required tipping over the applecart of conventional venture-funding wisdom. The adventure began in 2006 on an annual gambling pilgrimage to Las Vegas. Back then Starr was the 45-year-old CFO and Levin the 55-year-old biochemical engineer and CEO of Millennial Pharmaceuticals. Now, imagine the following scene in your mind: a scientist and a finance executive enter a gambling room at the Bellagio to play blackjack and re-emerge as biotech crusaders ready to take on the hyper-competitive drugs industry. The protagonists may not have worn superhero outfits but as they scrutinised their cards several factors weighed heavily on their minds. Venture funding for early-stage drug research had dried up, taking a gamble on a drug just doesn't promise returns as high as, say, investing in the next Instagram or Snapchat. On top of this, pharmaceutical companies were slashing their research and development. At the time, venture capitalists only funded ideas already in clinical trials. This meant many great ideas never found early-stage funding to get them to the crucial milestone of testing and they remained languishing in academic journals while federal grants funding promising academic research was being wasted.

Echoing what Peter Thiel was seeing as a lack of meaningful innovation, the three partners recognised the danger as well as the opportunity of no one betting on big life-science ideas. "Patients are getting screwed, we need to do something," said Starr. Levin agreed. Within their world of influence, doing something entailed disrupting the way in which drug companies and venture capitalists thought and to do this they would need to bring a new mindset to the party. As Levin put it, "If venture isn't investing in early stage, and Big Pharma isn't investing in early stage, there's going to be a big hole there," and it was this gaping hole in the biotech value chain that offered these three questers the opportunity to boldly go where others feared to. So Third Rock Ventures was born out of an idea to create meaningful benefits for the people who mattered the most within their world of influence – the patients. In order to be successful, their endeavour required changing the rules and the model for venture funding.

Their quest led them to explore academic research facilities where they found in Starr's own words "jaw-dropping innovations". But these ideas were not being progressed because of the industry's failing funding model. The partners of Third Rock believed they could offer a powerful combination of both funding and management expertise. Their strategy to disrupt the industry comprises four parts.

The first part of the strategy involves "finding the very best ideas and people in research and academia". This strategy requires launching a start-up business around scientific research and managing the business operations themselves until the business can be spun-off in IPOs. To do this, Levin and crew spend thousands of hours a year leading the drug companies they themselves have founded and funded. Preferring home-grown ideas, rather than ideas pitched to them means that Third Rock marches to a different tune from that of other venture capitalists. "Last year we saw 982 outside plans," says Starr. "We invested in zero."

The team at Third Rock launches five to seven new start-up ventures each year and is actively involved from the earliest stages of each business's development. At Third Rock they come up with breakthrough scientific ideas and then invest and manage the most promising of them. Third Rock partners take leadership positions in each start-up quest and they fund and put in thousands of leadership hours over 12 to 18 months before hiring professional managers to take the businesses forward to initial public offering.

This requires a different team from the accountants and investment-fund managers typically hired in the venture capital world. At Third Rock only Levin had worked in the venture capital sector prior to starting the business. Rather they hire battle-hardened peers who have done time in the scientific trenches as physicians, scientists and biotechnologists. The partners believe people make the difference when embarking on a quest to build companies seeking solutions for important unmet medical needs, so they only employ the very best. This often means delaying projects by months as candidates are interviewed.

Third Rock also believes in the power of group genius: "Individual genius is great," said Levin, "but drug development goes well beyond individual genius." The team at Third Rock invite leading scientific minds and business visionaries to working sessions where they brainstorm with the Third Rock crew to identify opportunities that will change the future of medicine. To this end, they operate a version of open-source idea generation. By working in collaboration with experts across the industry and in academia they are able to bring to market promising therapies and see to fruition home-grown ventures. Venture partners from Third Rock become part of the founding management teams and they work *in* the business rather than *on* the business. Third Rock's philosophy is simple, allow the CEO to focus on building the business and the idea rather than worrying about where the next round of funding will come from.

Despite their laid-back almost hippy-like attitudes, the three founders Levin, Starr and Tepper have a thorough almost draconian approach. "It's a bunch of nerds," says Mikhail Shapiro a former employee. "You're in a commercial setting, but the rigour of the science is as high as it is at MIT or Caltech." This rigour is a trait common in successful questers. A laser focus on *au courant* science and creating home-grown companies underpinned by mind-blowing ideas conceived by the Third Rock crew enables them to back larger-than-average investments – between $35 million to $45 million – up to six times more than the average biotech Series A investment by a venture capitalist.

The second part of Third Rock's strategy: "Do not pursue ideas that Big Pharma is already pursuing," involves strict adherence to the acronym TRUKK or Third Rock Ultra Killer Kriteria. Each investment has to meet three criteria and no exceptions are tolerated: the innovation must be no more than three years away from clinical trials; Big Pharma cannot be playing in or considering entering the innovation space being considered; and, key findings need to be replicated without any spikes in toxicity. Having passed these three hurdles, Third Rock moves into overdrive to implement its unique business model.

There is an important logic behind this part of the strategy. Big Pharma typically pursues large mass-market opportunities so this strategy achieves two things for Third Rock. Firstly, it creates a blue-ocean strategic opportunity by enabling the new start-up firm to focus on disruptive innovation that opens up new markets. Secondly, the company is able to develop therapies in a relatively unchallenged market and, once these innovations take hold, they can then be migrated upstream to challenge larger, more lucrative markets. It's classic disruptive blue-ocean strategy in action.

The third part of their strategy involves ensuring the developments will make a big difference in the lives of patients. Living a strategy that necessitates delivering meaningful benefits to the world, over and above making profits, is the single most important quality of a quest. Third Rock's world – where it has a direct and meaningful influence – is the world of the patient. An example of the company's commitment to this quest is demonstrated by the practice of inviting patients every three months to come talk to everyone in the company about living with rare diseases. "We always cry our eyes out and get fired up to go back to the office," says Starr.

On June 2011, motivated to make a difference and driven by their TRUKK criteria, Third Rock announced one of its most important ventures: the $26-million-dollar Series A financing deal launching Lotus Tissue Repair. The financing was used to advance a proprietary protein replacement therapy, being developed as a treatment for dystrophic epidermolysis bullosa or EB, the condition ravaging Rafi Kopelan's body. Two University of South California professors Dr David Woodley and Mei Chen had developed the technology. Being a treatment for a rare disease, Third Rock knew they would be safe from Big Pharma playing in that sector as the profit returns were too risky. However, the investors also knew that the promising treatment, which involves cloning the human gene that makes type VII collagen responsible for bonding the epidermis with the dermis together, had shown very promising preliminary results.

The strategy behind launching Lotus Tissue Repair was brilliant. Leverage the research of the two university professors and create meaningful benefits for Rafi and the EB community, thereby fulfilling Third Rock's quest to build great companies with the potential to make a dramatic difference in patients' lives. Then as the drug technology is perfected and proven, migrate upstream to disrupt more lucrative larger markets. Lotus Tissue Repair would then become an attractive acquisition option.

Third Rock's strategy worked. Applications for Lotus Tissue Repair's newly developed drug technology could also be applied for treatments in mass-market dermatological conditions, such as diabetic foot ulcers, venous stasis ulcers and other similar conditions. Eighteen months after the launch of Lotus Tissue Repair, Shire Pharmaceuticals a FTSE 100 biotech company originating in the United Kingdom with a market capitalisation of over £32,5 billion, announced the acquisition of Lotus for $49.3 million plus another $275 million if Lotus hit certain safety and development milestones. For its audacious investment Third Rock Ventures made a handsome immediate three-fold return and if the agreed milestones are reached, the big bet on Lotus will net a 20-fold return on investment.

"They're one of the few firms I've seen in 30 years that have reinvented the model of venture capital," says Bill Helman of Greylock Partners, a company that funded the explosive growth of Airbnb. The results have been spectacular and Third Rock has launched companies that deliver ground-breaking medical advances for diseases, which are increasingly having a big impact on society.

As money continues to flow out of life sciences, perhaps the best compliment to Third Rock is that other venture capital firms like Google Ventures, PureTech Ventures and the Longwood Fund are starting to replicate their model of investing in bold life-sciences ventures that deliver meaningful benefits. Rich Aldrich, a founding partner of Longwood Fund, was asked in an interview with the American newspaper *The Boston Globe*, "whether it wouldn't be easier to go develop a mobile app and hope that Facebook would acquire it for $1 billion." His response: "Once you've been involved in creating new medicines, other things don't seem quite as important."

Although life has presented Rafi with more challenges than other children, she goes through every day just like any other kid. "She laughs, she explores, she enjoys. She is truly amazing. It is a testament to her strength, her determination, her courage and her attitude. We can't get enough of her," says Rafi's father Brett. Thanks to the work of Third Rock and a band of vanguard venture questers, the Kopelans will hopefully soon spend more quality time with Rafi and the world will be waking up a better place.

Chapter Two

Perversions of the Proper Workings of Capitalism

"You never change things by fighting the existing reality. To change something, build a new model that makes the existing model obsolete."
Buckingham Fuller.

1.

Seth Godin, a business change evangelist tells a great joke that nails the paradox between business and society's needs in the 21st century on the head. It goes like this: "A woman visits her psychologist and says, *'Doctor, doctor my husband thinks he is a chicken!'* The psychologist says, *'That is terrible. Tell me, how long has he believed this?'* The woman says, *'Three-months...'* The psychiatrist shouts, *'THREE MONTHS! Why on earth didn't you come to see me sooner?'* The woman replies, *'Because we needed the eggs.'"*

2.

"The present state of affairs is really a perversion of the proper working of capitalism. It is all wrong to have billionaires before you have ceased to have slums. Capitalism has done enormous good and suits human nature far too well to be given up as long as human nature remains the same. But the perversion has given us too unstable a society." These are the words of Spedan Lewis, the founder of the John Lewis Partnership. I like what Spedan said about the "proper workings of capitalism" because he was right. Capitalism, when operating optimally, delivers significant and very meaningful benefits.

But here's the catch. We all know about the perversions of the industrial system that Spedan referred to, side effects like: pollution; income inequality; soul-destroying jobs; companies behaving unethically; bosses being disrespectful to employees or customers and being paid outrageous bonuses while there are people living in slums – but for the large part we've done little to change capitalism because we have wanted the "eggs". Like our grandparents and parents, we have accepted the industrialised mindset that has produced the organisations of our modern world. But at a personal cost – giving up control by working 9-to-5; conforming by not deviating from tasks set out in job descriptions; and, offering compliance by dressing and behaving as stipulated. In return, the industrial system has "rewarded" us with a lot of affordable shiny stuff. But as Godin concludes: "Just because you're winning a game doesn't make it a good game."

The current shareholder model of capitalism frequently fails to deliver sustainable and meaningful benefits to society and the world. In a paper for the Dallas Federal Reserve, economists calculated that "the total cost to the U.S. for the 2008 financial crisis was in the order of $6 trillion to $14 trillion." Breaking that down into recognisable terms, the price tag for the financial crisis just in the US, rises to as much as $120,000 for every man, woman and child. Imagine the meaningful benefits that would have accrued to education, health and sciences if this money had been put to better use than bank bailouts.

The Great Recession may be behind us but the aftershocks of this tidal wave of economic disruption are still pulsating through the global economy. The growing inequalities gap, Greek ruptures in the Eurozone, wars being fought with Islamic States, Syrian refugees flooding into Europe and burgeoning government debts are all symptoms of an economic system that benefits the few and is now worryingly in danger of ending in the type of societal disruption Spedan Lewis warned us of.

To turn this negative and disruptive tide around, the 21st century needs the growing might of ethically minded leaders on a quest to use business as a force for good by improving the world. It is here that the importance of being on a quest comes to the fore because quests by their very nature deliver meaningful benefits.

Leaders can gain sustainable competitive advantages by delivering meaningful benefits to the societies they serve, broader communities, and the world within their influence. Fortuitously a quiet revolution is surging, rapidly reaching tipping point. Do not miss this revolution because it is changing the future of how organisations work and will usher in a new era where a remodelled version of capitalism delivers more meaningful benefits to all stakeholders.

3.

"You never change things by fighting the existing reality. To change something, build a new model that that makes the existing model obsolete," are the astute words from American architect, designer and inventor Buckingham Fuller. Questers understand the importance of disrupting current paradigms by creating new models. The movement for a new more meaningful model of capitalism has the backing of some of today's most thoughtful leaders. Even the former champion of shareholder capitalism Jack Welch and the man voted by *Forbes* as the greatest manager of the 20th century, has recognised the failings of the capitalist shareholder model and, in doing so, become one of its strongest critics. Following the most recent global financial collapse Welch came out batting hard saying in an interview with Francesco Guerrera of the *Financial Times*, "On the face of it, shareholder value is the dumbest idea in the world. Shareholder value is a result, not a strategy. The main constituencies are your employees, your customers and your products. Managers and investors should not set share price increases as their overarching goal. Short-term profits should be allied with an increase in the long-term value of a company."

Small changes in the corporate code can change the world and on April 13, 2010, Governor Martin O'Malley made history in the US State of Maryland when he passed a law creating a new type of for-profit corporation – *the Benefit Corporation.* With a stroke of his pen O'Malley constituted the power of commerce to generate profit as well as deliver meaningful and positive benefits for society, employees and the environment.

A benefit corporation, in the simplest terms, is legally obligated to create benefits for both society and its shareholders. Had Spedan Lewis been alive today he is sure to have endorsed this new model as a way forward to tackle the perversions of the capitalist system he spoke about. This modern movement is driven by astute questers who recognise that delivering meaningful benefits to society can also generate significant competitive advantages. "It's going to take time for that to get organised," said Andrew Greenblatt from B Lab, a certification company, which consulted for the State of Maryland during the drafting of the benefit corporation legislation, "but 10 to 20 years from now this will be the standard way of doing business. And if you're not a benefit corporation people are going to ask why not."

To date 28 US states have joined the State of Maryland in passing benefit corporation legislation. The growth and development of the benefit corporation movement, is being supported by B Lab who offer independent certification to companies aiming to do well, by doing good. The B Lab certificate provides a recognisable label in much the same way the Fairtrade mark offers consumers an easily identifiable independent guarantee of a better deal for Third-World producers.

"The desire to balance profit and purpose is arguably a return to the model that many American companies once followed," says James Surowiecki, a journalist with *The New Yorker* magazine in an article he wrote about this exciting new development in capitalism's history. "Henry Ford declared that, instead of boosting dividends, he'd rather use the money to build better cars and pay better wages. And Johnson & Johnson's credo, written in 1943, stated that the company's 'first responsibility' was not to investors but to doctors, nurses, and patients."

Working in tandem, the B Lab certification and benefit corporation legislation is having a profound impact on the future of capitalism. "Corporations primarily create wealth for one group of people and don't add a lot of other value to society," says Andrew Kassoy from B Lab. "If we want to solve a lot of our big social and environmental problems, we need the private sector to play a role because it dominates our economy and fixing those problems requires scale." Leaders who wish to make a difference to the bottom line as well as deliver meaningful benefits to their co-workers, customers and society now have powerful statutory and certification frameworks that support this quest.

Benefit corporations or B Corps as B Lab calls them are required to meet rigorous standards of social and environmental performance, accountability and transparency. In turn, they are protected by legislation that gives directors a fiduciary responsibility to deliver meaningful benefits to society over and above profit. This is not a marketing gimmick or bandwagon to be jumped onto. By signing up to become a benefit corporation the directors and shareholders agree to greater degrees of transparency and accountability. If they fall short, for example, on social issues such as treating employees or the environment fairly, directors can be taken to court and sued. Conversely the legislation also protects directors who want to pursue social business practices from unscrupulous investors looking for a quick return. Businesses that switch to benefit corporation status have to be serious about the role they want to play in society and the legislation offers them protection from profiteering shareholders. Milton Friedman must be turning in his grave at the growing community of over 1,300 certified B Corps from 41 countries in over 121 industries that are working together towards one unifying quest: *to redefine success in business to deliver meaningful benefits for the people they work with and society.*

4.

"If you look at the history of business, I would say that's how we started," said Lesley Keil, a legal partner who advises leaders who want to legally convert to benefit corporation status. "But somewhere along the way, it became just about the bottom line, what your dividends are to shareholders, and what executives are taking home, rather than building a long-lasting business that enriches the community," she explains. The old paradigm of profit maximisation for shareholders is being replaced by a new paradigm that optimises profits through providing meaningful benefits to employees, customers and the world.

This new paradigm of doing well by doing good has stellar backing. Michael Porter, eminent professor of business strategy at the Harvard Business School says, "Companies are beginning to compete to change the world for the better. The drive for profit, often criticized for coming at society's expense, is driving and enabling solutions to many of the world's most challenging problems."

Industrial manufacturing giant GE is one of a vanguard of companies pushing the envelope of this new paradigm. GE has recognised the shift in competitive advantage and Jeff Immelt, GE's CEO has proclaimed a quest to *"improve the world by one percent every year"*. This audacious quest translates into trillions of dollars of meaningful benefits to the planet and GE's customers.

GE has recognised that growing computer power in a connected world is revolutionising the ability to gather massive amounts of data, process that data in real time and benefit immediately from valuable output. This is a game changer and those companies that miss this revolution will, Immelt believes, "be like those retailers who missed the Internet, it will be too late".

Behind this revolution is the Internet of Things, billions of tiny sensors connecting people, machines and objects to the Internet. According to Cisco, a computing company, by 2008 there were already more things connected to the Internet than people living on Planet Earth and by 2020 there will be over 50 billion things connected, interacting and contributing towards making the world smarter. The Internet of Things revolves around increased machine-to-machine and machine-human communication; it's built on cloud computing, advanced analytics, data-gathering sensors and intelligent machines. It is mobile, virtual, and instantaneous connection; and it's poised to revolutionise our everyday lives.

"The ability in our world to go man to machine, the ability to marry real-time customer data with real-time performance data of our products, to me that's the Holy Grail," Immelt says, explaining why it's important to GE's quest. By marrying intelligent machines, sensors, and real-time information, GE estimates they can help industries and the global economy to save trillions of dollars. GE is disrupting the global economy by moving from "productivity" to "predictivity". This clever play on two words – predict and productivity – captures GE's strategic quest to deliver meaningful and lasting benefits in industries such as aviation, healthcare, utilities, oil and gas. Savings are predicted to amount to $82 trillion over a 15-year period, which is equivalent to approximately half of the annual global economy.

GE provides some examples to demonstrate the power of one percent: fuel savings for aviation would yield an amount of $30 billion. Global gas-fired power plants would generate a $66-billion reduction in fuel consumption. The global healthcare industry would benefit by more than $63 billion in savings. Rail freight would gain $27 billion in fuel savings; and, a one percent improvement in capital utilisation in oil and gas exploration would total $90 billion in avoided or deferred capital expenditures.

As GE puts it "a little bit of savings goes a long way" and the meaningful benefits ratchet up very quickly.

It is increasingly clear that when quests form part of the organisation's core strategy, they have the greatest impact on change and value creation. Even business leaders like Immelt with a hard-nosed focus on the bottom line and demanding shareholders are embarking on quests to deliver meaningful benefits. From these strategies they are building sustainable competitive advantages that were not possible using the old capitalist mindset of shareholder value creation.

We are currently witnessing a massive paradigm shift in thought leadership in terms of what makes companies competitive as well as contributors to society. GE is not alone in embarking on quests that deliver meaningful benefits. Other switched-on corporate questers are catching the shift from shareholder to benefit-driven capitalism. This change is now progressing at full speed. In its September 2015 edition, *Fortune* magazine published its first list of organisations focusing on quests that deliver meaningful benefits. The *"Change the World List"* as *Fortune* magazine calls it "recognises this shift in competitive corporate strategy."

The magazine's editors have identified and ranked 51 mega corporations that are making a considerable impact on major global problems and delivering meaningful benefits to society as part of their core competitive strategy. *Fortune* magazine importantly identifies that doing well by doing good, "is not meant to be a ranking of the overall 'goodness' of companies or of their 'social responsibility.'" Rather they explain, "Big corporations are complex operations that affect the world in myriad ways. The goal is simply to shine a spotlight on instances where companies are doing good as part of their profit-making strategy, and to shed new light on the power of capitalism to improve the human condition."

Which brings us to corporate social responsibility. "Corporate leadership is not just about attracting investors; it's also about doing what's right for business. Current trends go beyond previous models of corporate social responsibility precisely because more companies see that a focus on social and environmental impact affects the bottom line," says Judith Rodin, the president of the Rockefeller Foundation and author of *The Power of Impact Investing*. Giving away a percentage of profit to charity does not go far enough and while it may be better than doing nothing, it continues to perpetuate an out-of-date shareholder model through the façade of good corporate citizenship.

Increasingly companies that are on quests to deliver meaningful benefits are going to end up making a lot of money. According to

Rodin, "the assets managed under socially responsible principles doubled to more than $6 trillion between 2012 and 2014." And, her study for the Rockefeller Foundation reveals that "almost half of all high-net-worth investors want to align more of their investments with their values." This figure rises among the Millennial Generation, whom I talk about in the next chapter. This cohort "will inherit more than $30 trillion over the next few decades and 92 percent believe that a business's purpose extends beyond profit."

Leaders now have a choice: continue to perpetuate the old capitalist paradigm or join a marvellous adventurous quest and become part of a new paradigm for creating sustainable competitive advantage, economic value and wealth that delivers meaningful benefits across society and the world.

Chapter Three

A Generation of Questers

"Kids can really change the world"
Taylor Wilson

1.

The generation born in the decades around the turn of the last century are called the Millennial Generation or Generation Y. They are the largest generation in history, larger than the Baby Boomers, and this cohort of young future revolutionaries is about to move into its prime spending years. They are also the first generation to grow up in a world where "digital" is normal and are poised to reshape the economy and future world of work.

Their unique approach is changing how we buy and sell, how we work and how we lead. According to Deloitte, a large management consultancy, by 2025 this generation will represent over 75 percent of the global workforce but few businesses are ready for the social disruption this energetic trailblazing generation is bringing to the work and marketplace. They are described as overly confident, bordering on arrogant. But from their perspective they just want to get the right results for a world in turmoil and believe other generations have the wrong outlook.

The Millennial Generation, as I will show, is without a shred of doubt a generation of questers on steroids! This is tremendously encouraging news because the world has an urgent need for ethically driven, morally minded questers to embark on quests that will drive meaningful benefit and make the world a better place.

Quests are second nature to Millennials; they have grown up watching epic Hollywood quests from *Avatar* to *Lord of the Rings* and playing a multitude of adventure quest-based games. Quests are inherently central to the values of this generation and they are growing up impatient to embark on their own world-changing adventures.

With the advantage of technology on their side, Millennial change agents are racing forward to deliver meaningful change in the world, and, very little can stop them, certainly not a stuffy organisation or leaders with outdated views on profits and organisational meaning. Overwhelmingly this generation believes that businesses are focused on their own agenda rather than helping to improve society. "Millennials want more from business than might have been the case 50, 20, or even 10 years ago," says Deloitte Global CEO, Barry Salzberg. "They are sending a very strong signal to the world's leaders that when doing business, they should do so with purpose. The pursuit of this different and better way of operating in the 21st century begins by redefining leadership." If organisations want to attract the best talent, they need to understand where they can add the most benefit to the society they touch and set course on quests to deliver meaningful differences. This goes far beyond products and profits.

This generation looks around and they see numerous examples of their own cohort starting ventures, many of which have become exceptionally successful. Take Theranos founder and CEO, Elizabeth Holmes (born 1984) who is a quester from the Millennial Generation. She is also the world's youngest self-made female billionaire. Holmes was always going to be a quester; at the age of nine, she wrote to her father saying: "What I really want out of life is to discover something new, something that mankind didn't know was possible," echoing the quest quality of making the impossible, possible.

Inspired by stories of her great-great-grandfather, Christian Holmes, a surgeon, Holmes enrolled at Stanford University to study medicine, but at the age of 19 she dropped out to work on Real-Time Cures, later rebranded, Theranos – the word comes from a combination of therapy and diagnose – in the basement of a college house. "When I realised this is what I wanted to do with my life, things got easy," Holmes told *USA Today*, "because when you reach that moment when you've found what you're born to do, well then you just got to do it."

Holmes tells the story of a diabetic woman who used a Theranos blood test and paid only $34 for the service. The woman said she had undergone the same tests earlier that year and that it cost her nearly $900. Holmes explains her overarching disruptive quest: "Theranos is enabling everyone, no matter how much money they have, or where they live, or what kind of insurance they have, to be able to have access to the kind of testing information that could change their lives. Actionable health information at the time it matters most," says Holmes, "is a basic human right." For ten years Holmes worked feverously below the radar developing 84 patents and launching an innovative minimal invasive blood test that requires only a pinprick on the finger but is capable of testing for medical conditions like cancer and high cholesterol. Like many of today's questers she recognises the power of democratised real-time information in disrupting even established industries overnight.

Theranos, now valued at $9 billion, is expanding into 8,400 stores of Walgreen, the largest drug retailer in the United States and provides test results within 24 hours. Holmes's 50 percent stake in Theranos means she is now worth $4.5 billion. And, it all started out by, "thinking about what is the greatest change I could make in the world." By embarking on a quest to deliver meaningful benefits, Elizabeth Holmes is a quester extraordinaire!

Another well-known Millennial quester is Mark Zuckerberg (also born in 1984), the CEO billionaire and Founder of Facebook. Zuckerberg is on a quest to connect the world. Connecting the first billion was easy; the next five billion is what Zuckerberg has his eye on. It would be flippant to argue that all Millennials are interested in is the riches that might follow. Millennials have no issues with making money and being rich, but first and foremost they want their work to deliver meaningful benefits to the world. Deloitte's study revealed that up to 77 percent of Millennials choose to work for their current employer because the company has a purpose that makes a difference in the world. If they do not find a meaningful difference with an existing business, members of this generation fearlessly embark on their own meaningful quests and start their own organisations. As an archetypal Millennial, Zuckerberg provides unpolished insights into what a future world of work dominated by Millennial values and behaviours might look like.

For example, he was severely criticised by Wall Street when he paid a massive $19 billion to acquire WhatsApp, a mobile messaging service with nearly half a billion users worldwide and growing at one million users a day. Jan Koum, the co-founder of WhatsApp, had openly distanced his company from ever selling adverts. Zuckerberg's quest, however, is bigger than selling adverts, so he sat down with Koum and explained his quest to connect the world and proposed they work together. "Eleven days ago, last Sunday evening, I said if we joined together it would really connect the rest of the world. He thought about it and over the course of the week he said he was interested ... then we got the price later in the week and came to terms," explained Zuckerberg to shareholders. This demonstrates two important things. Firstly, the way Millennials work and secondly, that the quest was always more important than the price; it's what swung the negotiation between Koum and Zuckerberg. A big cheque book does not impress Millennials questers unless it is supported by a quest that delivers meaningful benefits to the world. The terms agreed commercially favoured WhatsApp over Facebook, but that didn't matter because the acquisition was part of a larger more important quest. Koum explained to investors, "Monetisation is not going to be a priority for us. Zuckerberg focuses on things five or 10 years from now. So in 2020, or 2025, five billion people will have a smartphone and we will have a potential for five billion users." Ultimately Zuckerberg believes that giving people more information about the lives of people around them "should create more empathy", and that makes a better world, which is worth joining forces for and questing towards.

In an interview with *Wired Magazine*, Zuckerberg captures the essence and importance of his quest and how he is using the Facebook model as a vehicle for changing the world for the better. "The story of the next century is the transition from an industrial, resource-based economy, to a knowledge economy. An industrial economy is a zero sum game. If you own an oil field, I cannot go in that same oil field. But knowledge works differently. If you know something, then you can share that – and then the whole world gets richer. But until that happens, there's a big disparity in the wealth. The richest 500 million have way more money than the next six billion combined. You solve that by getting everyone online, and into the knowledge economy – by building out the global Internet."

Peter Thiel is one of Zuckerberg's mentors and is a member of the Facebook Board. He knows that future competitive advantage comes from businesses focusing on doing more for society. He says, "What I like about the Facebook model is it is centred on real human beings... globalisation doesn't mean you are friends with everybody in the world. But it somehow means that you are open to a lot more people in a lot more contexts than you would have been before." No doubt Thiel had an influence in Zuckerberg's negotiations with Koum.

If you give people a better way to share information you change the world. History demonstrated this with the invention of the printing press; it is seeing it again in this digitally-connected-information-democratised era.

2.

Started in 2011, the *Thiel Fellowship* is a learning and development platform for questers that brings, "together some of the world's most creative and motivated young people, and helps them bring their most ambitious projects to life." Its founder Peter Thiel recognised that if you want to change the world – or your organisation – you need to create the supporting structures, models and platforms that will support new paradigms and new thinking. His philosophy behind the fellowship asks an important question, "Why let school get in the way of learning?"

It's important to help questers break free from the 3Cs of management – control, conformity and compliance. These are the three shackles holding the hare back in the race for competitiveness in the 21st century. "Nothing forces us to funnel students into a tournament that bankrupts the losers and turns the winners into conformists," Thiel wrote in *The Washington Post*. "But that's what will happen until we start questioning whether college is our only option."

The Thiel Fellowship is challenging conventional wisdom and operates on the following three principles: two years spent developing meaningful quests; $100,000 of commitment-free seed capital. And, because "some ideas just can't wait," controversially the Silicon Valley investor encourages fellows to chase breakthrough technologies that change the world instead of wasting their time and money in college. According to the fund's website, Thiel's fellows have "produced more than $200 million in economic activity… started 58 organizations…with an aggregate value of more than half a billion dollars." Thiel's quest to reignite the growth of global innovations, in areas of health, engineering and sciences – which in his view are suffering from severe stagnation – is making good headway.

Many of the fellows are pioneering completely new concepts and as their quests unfold they aim to deliver meaningful benefits to the world. I've taken a few names from the most recent crop of Thiel's questers to illustrate the adventurous quests that this ambitious generation are following:

Twenty-two-year-old Harry Gandhi is on a quest to create a smart contact lens for "continuous and non-invasive monitoring of health vitals, starting with diabetes management".

Eighteen-year-old Cathy Tie, the co-founder and CEO of Ranomics, a biotech startup, is on a quest to "revolutionise preventative medicine by determining with unparalleled precision whether a person is prone to a hereditary condition as a result of their individual genetic variations".

Nineteen-year-old Jeremy Cai is on a quest to reinvent how organisations build a modern workforce by developing software to streamline and automate interactions with service providers. He is the founder and CEO of OnboardIQ.

At 17 years of age, Jihad Kawas from Beirut is one of the youngest fellows. Kawas's quest is to help build neighbourhoods that don't waste. He is founder and CEO of Saily, an online local marketplace that helps neighbours buy, sell, and swap second-hand products using their mobile phones.

Ocean Pleasant also 17, founded *REAL* Magazine, a national youth culture publication dedicated to engaging Millennials on questions of social change.

Millennials think big and their quests reflect this. All the fellows have different ideas and come at things from different angles but they have one thing in common – they are on quests to deliver meaningful benefits that will change the world.

But perhaps it is Taylor Wilson a self-assured 21-year-old, who is the most famous of Thiel's fellows. Taylor shot to stardom when at the tender young age of 14; he became the youngest individual to build a nuclear fusion reactor. He had been pestering his parents to create a fusion reactor for some time. They relented and took him to meet revered physicist Friedwardt Winterberg at the University of Nevada. The professor was stunned and unimpressed, "You're thirteen years old!" One can almost imagine the "Doh!" that raced through Taylor's mind as the professor waxed on lyrically, "and, you want to play with tens of thousands of electron volts and deadly x-rays? First you must master calculus, the language of science." Tiffany and Kenneth Wilson, Taylor's parents breathed a momentarily sigh of relief hoping against hope that the professor's analysis would take the wind out of Taylor's sails, or at least delay him until he went to university. But as Kenneth now says that was always highly unlikely, "Taylor doesn't understand the meaning of 'can't'." Tiffany concurs adding, "and when he does, he doesn't listen." In classic Millennial, "speak to the hand because the face ain't listening" Taylor went into overdrive, which is also not a surprise because he is a quester and the slightest suggestion that his quest was impossible, further turbocharged his ambitions.

Taylor believed his fusion reactor could deliver meaningful benefits in the areas of medical health. His grandmother had died of cancer and he wondered if the isotopes from a "fusor", as he called his reactor, might help to make diagnosing cancer cheaper and easier to perform. Taylor met atomic physicist Ronald Phaneuf when he visited Professor Winterberg but unlike his esteemed colleague Phaneuf was impressed with the Young Turk. Phaneuf shares a story where he tells how Taylor, "told me he wanted to build a nuclear reactor in his garage, and I thought, 'Oh my lord, we can't let him do that. But maybe we can help him try to do it here'... He had a depth of understanding I'd never seen in someone that young." Phaneuf quickly cleared a space at his lab where Taylor subsequently spent every afternoon after school fabricating his fusor. Shortly after his 14th birthday, Taylor became the 32nd individual in history to build a functioning nuclear fusion reactor.

But the fusion reactor was not the end destination and the quest is not complete: "I want to play major league, I want to make a difference." Taylor continues his quest experimenting and patenting innovative ways to use his small fusors in hospitals to make medical isotopes easily available for the diagnosis and treatment of cancer. His innovations may soon reach thousands of patients especially those in poor countries where access to isotopes is either too expensive or too difficult to obtain.

"It's amazing – *amazing* – what I can do today," says Taylor, "that I couldn't have done if I was born 10 years earlier." Perhaps this is one of the reasons why the Millennial generation are a generation of questers. They understand intuitively the technology available today and how it can be leveraged in innovative ways to change the world. However, you do not need to come from the Millennial generation to be a quester; it's just that older generations have more baggage to get rid of in order to unlearn. Millennials have at their fingertips an understanding of what new technology can do and they are not stuck in a rut tainted by current paradigms that say this or that is impossible.

After finishing his Thiel Fellowship, Taylor admits he still has no plans to go to university. "I've got some technology that will really change the world, so college right now is not the best option for me," he says. His biggest dream is to solve the world's energy problems, a huge and meaningful quest. Just don't tell Taylor it's impossible. I wouldn't bet against him. In fact, I wouldn't bet against *any* questers from this generation.

Part Two

The Power of Achieving the Impossible

"Elites aren't defined by birth or wealth, they are people with a project, individuals who want to do work they believe in, folks seeking to make an impact."
Seth Godin

Chapter Four

The Greatest Scientific Quest of the 21st Century

"New ideas emanate from the scary edges of society, not from the conservative centre"
Joel Kurtzman

1.

An overnight train heading east from Moscow into the central Volga region of Russia brings you to the secretive and sanctified town of Sarov. Surrounded by endless woodlands, the single-track railway line enters the town's station. Passengers disembark onto a platform guarded by soldiers and enter the town through locked metal gates ornamented with razor-sharp barbed wire. A billboard near the station proudly proclaims: "Sarov – Centre of Russia's Strength and Spirit".

Once the site of the sixth largest orthodox monastery and visited by Tsar Nicholas II in 1903, the monastery was closed following Bolshevik repressions. After World War Two, Sarov disappeared from Soviet maps and this secretive provincial town became known as "the Installation". To this day it is the centre of Russia's nuclear industry and the birthplace of her atomic bomb. "Here, people simultaneously pray for peace throughout the world and make things that can blow that very same world to pieces," says Pavel Busalayev, a prominent painter of religious icons.

Andrei Sakharov, the father of the Soviet H-Bomb, worked at the Installation. Although he "was at the forefront of the effort to build the most destructive weapons in history", according to American physicist Sidney Drell, "he eventually came to understand the dangers such weapons posed and became a courageous activist for peace and disarmament." Sakharov was not alone on his journey into dissent. Nuclear physicists on both sides of the Pacific pond began to understand the horrifying dangers their work had created and tried to lessen them.

By the late sixties as Sakharov's conscience and awareness of Soviet atrocities grew, he became vocal regarding the dangers of nuclear shadow boxing with the West and human rights violations in the USSR. His open and vocal protest of the Soviet invasion of Afghanistan in 1979 resulted in the KGB branding him a traitor, stripping him of all his scientific awards, arresting and forcing him into internal exile in the closed city of Gorky. Banned from receiving visitors, Sakharov was regularly harassed, tied to his bed and force-fed when he went on hunger strikes.

In 1986, following Perestroika reforms, Gorbachev called him back to Moscow and out of exile. "He was a pure theorist who invented the Soviet H-Bomb and, 20 years later, transformed into the foremost human-rights advocate and opponent of the Soviet regime," says Gennady Gorelik a journalist with *Scientific American.* "He put forward a powerful political principle: Never trust a government that doesn't trust its own people."

During the early years of the Cold War, however, Sakharov was sent to work at the Installation, where he initially said he saw himself as a "soldier in this new scientific war". One day in 1949 he was summoned to Moscow by Lavrentiy Beria, chief of the Soviet security and secret police, the man who Stalin introduced to US President Franklin D. Roosevelt at the Yalta Conference as "his Himmler". In Beria's waiting room he found Oleg Lavrentiev, a young sailor in the Pacific Fleet, who had boldly written to Stalin and the Central Committee about ideas he had on how to build a hydrogen bomb and what a controlled thermonuclear reaction might hold for future energy productions. Sakharov had already reviewed Lavrentiev's proposal and was now questioned by Beria in a manner he said "verged on the ingratiating." Sakharov understood that Lavrentiev had "raised an issue of immense significance, and had displayed initiative and creativity that merited all the possible support and aid." Furthermore he noted being, "greatly impressed by the originality and boldness of those ideas that were produced independently, long before any publications."

Lavrentiev's proposal, said Sakharov, was the spark for the first "vague ideas on magnetic thermal insulation." Sakharov had been pondering the problem of how to control a thermonuclear reaction – the process that powers our sun and stars – for some time. At temperatures exceeding 150 million degrees centigrade, there was no possible way the electrostatic confinement Lavrentiev proposed, would prevent the hot plasma from coming into contact and obliterating any surface it touched. However, as he read the proposal, Sakharov began to imagine that magnetic confinement rather than electrostatic confinement might solve the problem and the design for a magnetic thermonuclear energy reactor or Tokomak was born.

2.

"From the beginning people realised the huge payoff of fusion energy and they underestimated the difficulty, which perhaps was a good thing because when you set out on a quest, if you think it's as difficult as this has been, you might not set out," says Steven Cowley, CEO of the UK Atomic Energy Authority when I met with him at a decommissioned English navy airfield in Oxfordshire, now the centre for nuclear research in the UK. Cowley leads the Joint European Torus or JET facility at the Culham Centre for Fusion Energy. JET is currently the world's largest Tokomak fusion reactor, positioning Cowley near the epicentre of the most exciting scientific challenge of the 21st century.

"It all comes back to $E=mc^2$," says Cowley, who together with scientists and engineers from around the world are collaborating on a quest to create fusion energy. The collaboration has an unlikely birthplace. Emerging from midst of the Cold War, Gorbachev suggested to Reagan during the 1986 Geneva Summit that the two countries collaborate on a quest to create fusion energy for all of humankind.

This audacious scientific quest aims to create and sustain a burning miniature star on earth. Cowley explains, "In the middle of a star you've got quite a lot of hydrogen bumping into the other hydrogen at great velocity. The hydrogen nucleus is positively charged and so it will mostly bounce off another one. But if you fire them at each other really powerfully, and they hit dead on, they get close enough that the 'strong force', which binds the nucleus together, grabs them and fuses them. This releases lots of energy, keeping the star hot." If they can control a fusion burn then the heat can be harnessed to operate steam turbines that, in turn, generate electricity.

When Cowley and his international colleagues crack the code for fusion energy, they will have found the solution to all of humanity's energy requirements. Energy touches every aspect of modern-day life, so this is a quest with enormous implications for the future. Oil and fossil fuels have driven the might of industrial development for the past 200 years. Cowley says that oil has been a gift to humans. "Basically you stick a pipe in the ground and it pumps itself out; it's hugely efficient." He says, "You can see those famous pictures, oil gushing out like a gift to humans. Fossil fuels are stored for billions of years, under pressure so that you can easily get them, and we're going to use them up in the blink of an eye." In terms of the earth's and humanity's existence, the time we're going to spend burning fossil fuels is for a century or two at best.

Fusion energy, when we have it, will change the future. Fusion emits zero pollutants, is carbon free and burns nothing but hydrogen nucleuses. The process uses a mixture of the exotically sounding tritium and deuterium also known as heavy hydrogen. Deuterium is believed to be a remnant of the Big Bang and is one of two stable isotopes of hydrogen. It is found in natural abundance in the earth's oceans.

Here is what really catches attention and explains why fusion energy will be a huge paradigm shift – in a single litre of seawater there are 1.03×10^{22} atoms of deuterium. Translated, this means that if all the deuterium atoms in only one cubic kilometre of seawater were fused to form heavier atoms, then the energy released would be equivalent to that released from burning 1,360 billion barrels of crude oil. Astonishingly, this is approximately the total amount of oil originally present on this planet! Put differently, half a tub of bathwater and the amount of lithium contained in your laptop battery can provide enough fusion fuel to fuel all your energy needs for the next 30 years. There is enough deuterium in our oceans to fuel the insatiable energy appetite of 10 billion people living on our planet for the next 30 million years. Fusion energy is massively efficient and incredibly powerful, making this quest one of the most awe-inspiring and meaningful quests in the history of humanity.

The biggest challenge in making fusing energy a viable and alternative source to fossil fuels is achieving a sustainable fusion burn. This is the enormous mountain facing fusion questers like Cowley and one they've been collectively and individually attempting to solve for over 60 years.

Nuclear fission, the process that powers our nuclear power stations, involves splitting an atom and once started, kicks off a chain reaction that is hard to stop – something Chernobyl and Fukushima are testaments to. Fusion, the forcing together of two atoms, however, goes contrary to the natural laws of physics. Positive atoms repel each other so creating fusion on earth is inherently unnatural. This is fortunate because the fusion process at the centre of a star creates a very hostile environment. "We only put one-tenth of a gram of fuel in at any one time. If it all burns in a big burst at once, it's just nothing. Fusion is intrinsically safe," says Cowley and it "produces energy without making long-lived radioactive waste, or without emitting carbon."

To overcome fusion's biggest challenge and make the impossible, possible, the next phase in the quest has already commenced. This is headed up by an organisation known as ITER, pronounced "eat-er". ITER is an acronym for the International Thermonuclear Experimental Reactor. The word ITER also means "the way" in Latin. This international collaboration is funded and run by seven member entities – the EU, India, Japan, South Korea, China and the United States. Together these regions represent 65 percent of the global population.

ITER, Like JET, is based on the Tokomak concept of thermonuclear magnetic confinement invented by Sakharov in the 1950s. The organisation is located at Cadarache, a picturesque area in southern France, near Aix-en-Provence, better known for its lavender fields. Over the next decade, the largest, most complex and most expensive machine ever built, will come to life. Once completed, this colossus of a monument to humankind's hunger for energy may well surpass the Pyramids of Giza as a symbol of humankind's greatest achievements.

ITER is huge in terms of ambition and sheer scale. When completed, the Tokomak will stand 30 metres high and be 30 metres wide; it will weigh 23,000 tons – three times more than the Eiffel Tower.

Ten thousand tons of magnets will work together to confine and shape the burning miniature star held captive inside. They will generate a magnetic field 200,000 times higher than anything found on Earth. The enclosed cavernous vacuum vessel will be twice as large and 16 times heavier than the JET Tokomak.

Inside ITER's Tokomak will be a super-charged pressurised cloud of heavy hydrogen. The mixture of deuterium and tritium will be bombarded with electric currents and laser beams so powerful they will make lightning look like a tiny arc of static electricity. A supersized refrigerator or cryostat will surround the machine preventing it from overheating and being vaporised as the 200-million-degree plasma trapped inside rotates faster than the speed of sound in a continuous fusion burn.

The grounds alone surrounding the ITER Tokomak fusion reactor and containing all the buildings necessary for supporting, controlling and managing scientific experiments will cover more than 60 football pitches. When completed. ITER will generate 500MW of power while needing 50MW of power to operate. Scientists from all over the world are collaborating at ITER to work towards the quest of "harnessing the energy produced by the fusion of atoms to help meet mankind's energy needs".

Cowley believes that ITER and JET are too big and he compares today's fusion machines with the early days of flight, "I'm pretty certain we don't know how to do fusion in the optimum way. At the beginning of flight it was clear that airships were not an effective way to fly people around but very quickly the technology improved, planes became smaller, faster and more efficient." Cowley sees a similar innovation process happening with fusion as what happened with flight technology. We'll explore more about this in Chapter Ten.

There are critics in politics and the energy industry, representing the old paradigm, who would prefer for fusion never to happen. Because when it does the questers at the forefront of this technology will disrupt how energy is created. "It's hard to have a revolutionary organisation that's funded by governments," says Cowley when he shares some of the challenges the quest faces. "The time frames we're interested in are not political time frames."

Proving a sustainable fusion burn is possible will come at a cost of $15 billion. It's a cost that some politicians argue is too high. Let's put things into perspective, though, the Great Recession cost the global economy several trillion eye-watering dollars; and, according to CNN reports the cost of the United States' latest F-35 fighter jet comes in at over $400 billion. ITER's costs are a drop in the ocean in comparison, so why do some politicians argue and hamper progress? Because it appears there is considerable vested interest in the current energy paradigm. "There's a lot of money to be made," Cowley explains. "The world energy market is seven trillion a year, a few percent of that and you're a very, very wealthy individual. Fossil fuels are eighty percent of energy and eighty percent of seven trillion is a lot of cash." TomorrowToday predicts that the first quester to invent a scaled-down version of a fusion power device accessible to every home will become the world's first trillionaire. That is a large incentive to questers in this field of science because along with doing good for the planet they can do well financially too.

Before this happens though, ITER needs to prove that a fusion burn can be sustained; that's the scientific quest Cowley and cohorts are on. "I want to be there," he says. "That will happen in my lifetime, and it will be the defining moment for fusion... We've driven the system and we got fusion to happen [at JET which is now the prototype for ITER]. But a burn is when the fusion produces enough heat to keep itself hot so that it keeps on burning. When that happens, it will be the historic moment in the science of fusion. It's like getting a fire to light. You can put a match to fuel and while the match is alight things will burn, but it's not alive until you can take the match away and the flame continues," says Cowley.

To date the closest anyone has come to a sustained fusion burn is at JET. In 1997, Cowley and his team of scientists achieved a reaction of 16MW of fusion power produced from an input power of 24MW. The fusion energy gain was factor of around 0.7, a world record. A fusion energy gain factor – known as Q – of greater than one is required to achieve "breakeven". This is where the amount of energy produced equals the amount of energy consumed. JET's record proved a lot; they had lit the match but there was no sustained burn. Cowley believes they can improve on this and get closer to the breakeven point. "We hope in the next runs of JET that we'll approach a gain of one. But that's no good for energy production – you need a gain of 10, 20, 30 – much more energy coming than you put in. That's what ITER will do."

"ITER will not only produce more energy than it puts in, it will also get to a state where you don't have to put any energy in at all," says Cowley. In David MacKay's book *Sustainable energy without the hot air* he says about nuclear fusion that: "There's enough deuterium to supply every person in a ten-fold increased world population with a power of 30,000 kWh per day. That's more than 100 times the average American consumption for one million years." Duarte Borba, a scientific advisor argues, "It is this potential that justifies the cost of the fusion programme."

The quest for fusion energy is the defining quest in the 21st century. It requires bold leadership, unwavering nerve and resilience against politicians and the old energy regime who want to protect the current state of play. But with organisations like ITER, and scientists like Cowley and many others at the helm, the future for creating a star on Earth looks bright. There is possibly only one quest out there for humans to tackle that is bigger than fusion energy says Cowley, "If we ever figured out how to stop aging, that would be a bigger quest than fusion; suddenly people live forever. But above that, well, we won't produce energy in the future by almost any other method than fusion; it's just so obviously a better way to produce energy."

By 2050, fusion should be connected to the electricity grid and billions of people around the world will benefit from the clean carbon-free energy technology that Sakharov invented almost a hundred years before. The quest for fusion energy may have taken longer than anticipated and while there are those who believe fusion will never happen, achieving the impossible is the ultimate aim of a leader's quest and a source of great motivation. Accomplishing something impossible fuels the passion of talented questers, so it seems fitting that Sakharov, the father of the Tokomak, has the final say: "A thermonuclear reaction – the mysterious source of the energy of sun and stars, the substance of life on earth but also the potential instrument of its destruction – was within my grasp. It was taking shape at my desk. But I feel confident in saying that infatuation with a spectacular new physics was not my primary motivation; I could easily have found another problem in theoretical physics to keep me amused. What was most important for me at the time was the conviction that our work was essential."

Chapter Five

The Greatest Scientific Quest of the 18th Century

"Galileo Galilei, Christiaan Huygens and Sir Isaac Newton all grappled with it as a puzzle that seemed insoluble."
Dava Sobel

1.

"Let your children be fatherless and your wife a widow," the sailor cursed Admiral Sir Cloudlesy Shovel who, legend has, ordered him hung for inciting mutiny. The sailor's crime, keeping a record of the fleet's location, was punishable by death and by desperately forewarning the admiral of his navigator's error, the sailor revealed his surreptitious misconduct. The year was 1707 and the admiral and Commander-in-Chief of the Royal Navy's Mediterranean fleet was returning from engagements in the War of Spanish Succession. As he led a squadron of 21 battle-hardened ships sailing towards England, fresh from their bombardment of Toulon, the admiral was no doubt heady with success. He pictured a speedy return and felt confident that they would soon be receiving a hero's welcome.

But the fleet had left its return rather late and as the ships sailed north, they met with autumnal conditions, hazy fog, which Sir Cloudesley called "dirty weather". He made an observation for the first time in many days on 21 October and the following day, with soundings at 90 fathoms, Sir Cloudesley brought the fleet to a layby at about 12 o'clock. He summoned all the ship masters – the navigators of the fleet – aboard his flagship vessel *HMS Association*, a 96-gun second-class ship-of-the-line and consulted regarding their actual position. All the navigators except one – the master of Sir William Jumper's ship the *Lenox*, who calculated their position as being within three hours' sail of the Isles of Scilly – were of the opinion the fleet were nearer Ushant, an island off France. Sir Cloudesley agreed with group consensus: open waters lay ahead. Anchors were ordered raised late afternoon and the fleet set sail once again with *HMS Association* leading, followed closely by the *Eagle, Romney, St. George, Royal Ann,* and *Firebrand.* As the night fell, the fog gave way to stormy gale-force winds that lashed against the wooden vessels, creaking straining masts and whipping the sails. Then, without warning, *HMS Association* and her squadron of ships juddered across the Outer Gilstone Rock, a treacherous reef lying off the Isles of Scilly in the English Channel. With what must have been a sickening and frightening crash the ships were ripped apart by an unforgiving and unyielding force. The cursed Sir Cloudesley may have had just enough time to reflect on "killing the messenger", for the sailor had been right about the fleet's position.

The exact number of sailors to lose their lives in this disaster is unknown but with *HMS Association* losing all and having a complement of 900 sailors and marines, the total for the sunken ships is considered to be close to 2,000 souls lost at sea, one of the English Navy's worst naval disasters.

2.

Knowing one's position on the high seas requires two very simple but essential coordinates: latitude and longitude. Latitude reveals how far north or south of the equator you are. For centuries, navigators using the height of the sun had been capable of finding their latitude at sea. In contrast, determining longitude, which reveals how far around the world one has travelled from the original departure point, perplexed the greatest minds for centuries.

Determining longitude became the greatest scientific quest of the 18th century. The nation that discovered a solution for the perplexing problem would rule the waves and benefit from incredible economic riches. The British parliament charted this endeavour's importance: "Such a Discovery would be of particular advantage to the trade of Great Britain, and very much for the honour of this Kingdom." To encourage the best minds to channel energy, capital and resources towards achieving this quest, the British parliament passed the Longitude Act during the reign of Queen Anne on 8 July 1714. The act powerfully captured the importance of the quest to solve the longitude problem: "That nothing is so much wanted and desired at Sea, as the Discovery of the Longitude, for the Safety and Quickness of Voyages, the Preservation of Ships and the Lives of Men." To encourage the land's best thinkers to join the quest to find a longitude solution, a handsome prize of £20,000, worth nearly £3 million today, was offered as motivation.

Longitude and latitude is a topic I recall being taught at primary school. Longitude ran vertically north and south meeting at the poles, whereas latitude lay on the parallels horizontally circumnavigating the globe east and west. The expectation of my teacher was for me to remember which was which when it came to exam time. This seemingly innocuous requirement appeared to be a quest in itself for my teacher, who endeavoured to drum it into the impenetrable heads of my bored schoolmates by asking the longitude-latitude question in every geography test we wrote that year. To assist with this examinable quest my parents bought me a state-of-the-art illuminating world globe. I was captivated; with a flick of the switch the world came to life. At night time, long after I was meant to be asleep I'd turn on the globe and scan the glowing continents seeking exotic destinations by following the lines of latitude and longitude with my finger and imagining new adventures of unexplored domains. Little did I know at the time, and perhaps this information escaped my erudite teacher too, but the incredible stories of the people behind the quest to find a navigational solution to the longitude challenge would've made learning and remembering the topic significantly more interesting.

On the face of it the longitude challenge appears extremely simple. Our planet earth takes 24 hours to complete a 360-degree revolution and can therefore be subdivided into 24 segments of one hour with each hour representing a plus or minus 15 degrees change in longitude, depending on whether you are moving east or west. By knowing the local times at two points on earth at the same moment, a simple calculation determines current longitude. The vexing problem for ancient mariners, however, was the inability to tell the exact time at the meridian or their point of departure. Navigators of the period could easily measure the local time wherever they were by observing the sun, but they were unable to determine the time at some reference point, for example Greenwich, because a seafaring clock with the degree of accuracy required had not yet been invented. Precise pendulum clocks existed in the 17th century, but the motions of a ship plus vicissitudes in temperature and moisture prevented pendulum clocks from keeping accurate time at sea. Of course today with modern timepieces keeping time is not a problem, but in the 18th century navigating longitude using clocks seemed an impossible feat.

Even in recent living memory only the most expensive watches kept reliable time. Back in the seventies growing up as a child I remember having a wind-up watch that would systematically gain or lose minutes every day. I was not alone. My friends and I would strive for the bragging privileges of owning a watch that told the correct time. For a period this contest became so competitive that as soon as the bell for the end of school chimed we'd race our bicycles home and the first thing we'd do is grab the landline telephone – remember there were no mobile phones back then – and dial the free-call "time-of-the-day" number. Listening intently to hear the monotone voice of marching time: "When you hear the beep, the exact time will be...'two fifty-five and twenty seconds'...BEEP."

Sometimes, as petulant kids do, we'd redial the number several times to double even triple check, perhaps wondering or hoping some higher force had pushed time forwards or backwards. These were the days, after all, when Marty McFly's *Back to the Future* made young schoolboys dream that time travel was indeed possible. Of course the voice meticulously marched out the sands of time and we never caught it out. Watches and time-exactness bragging rights would be reset and the next day's "time feuds" started all over again.

The story behind the quest for longitude is brilliantly accounted for in Dava Sobel's book *Longitude*, so it is not the task of *Quest* to explore the story of the search for longitude, but rather to share the lessons we can extract from "the greatest scientific quest of that age". It is sobering to reflect, as Sobel points out, that the voyages made by ancient mariners during the entire Age of Exploration were undertaken without a single sailor knowing where he was. Brave captains and their crew relied on steadfast seamanship, the accuracy of latitude readings and the luck of dead reckoning. Consequently they consistently faced the risks of shipwreck or exhausting provisions before reaching their destinations.

Newton, Galileo, Halley and countless other brilliant minds tackled the quest for longitude and failed to forge workable solutions. In the book *Gulliver's Travels,* written by Anglo-Irish writer Jonathan Swift and published in 1726, Gulliver imagines himself living so long that: "I should then see the Discovery of the Longitude, the perpetual Motion, the Universal Medicine, and many other great Inventions brought to the utmost Perfection". To Swift, cracking the longitude code seemed about as impossible as the other marvels on the list. Sobel herself wrote that the quest for longitude "became a synonym for attempting the impossible".

3.

When Maximilian Büsser, the CEO of Maximilian Büsser & Friends (MB&F), a Swiss watch manufacturer, presented his latest prototype to his team he said, "You know what, I don't think anyone will ever buy this." They went ahead anyway, it took three years and three million dollars of investment to design and engineer the horological machine or HM4 Thunderbolt as the timepiece is known. "My team looked at me as if I was crazy, and we did it," says Maximilian. Launched in 2010 each timepiece had a price tag of $158,000. MB&F crafted around 100 HM4 models over the next three years with eager retailers and customers snapping up every one. The final edition of HM4, limited to eight timepieces, sold for $230,000 each, meaning in total MB&F

realised a five-fold return on investment. Not bad for a crazy idea that no one would buy.

Now 10 years into his self-proclaimed "adventure" Büsser looks back with pride on a journey that for all rational intents and purposes should never have happened. In an interview with *Luxurious Magazine* he said, "But of course all that was impossible. But it became an obsession and soon I just had to do it. Winston Churchill said about winning the Battle of Britain 'We did not know it was impossible, so we did it'. That is exactly what happened with MB&F. If I had asked anyone in the Industry, he would have advised me to forget about it."

We can start to see that being a quester requires identifying the trends, patterns and opportunities to do things that on the face of it appear crazily impossible – to other people that is, but not the quester. Increasingly, we are seeing businesses skyrocket from nowhere into market-dominant positions by creating disruptive business models that frankly on paper appear nuts. Point in case; imagine listening to a pitch by Brian Chesky, the founder and CEO of Airbnb, when he approached venture capitalists for a first round of funding. Chesky was looking for $150,000 for a 10 percent stake in his business. Of the seven venture capitalists he approached, five rejected the opportunity outright and two never even had the decency to come back with an answer. But then let's be fair to these investors, who in their right mind would invest in a business model that as legendary investor Fred Wilson now remorsefully says, "We couldn't wrap our heads around air mattresses on the living room floors as the next hotel room and did not chase the deal." Today a disheartened Wilson knows that the 10 percent that was on offer is valued at $2.5 billion – his team passed on Airbnb's early financing round. Airbnb have rocketed to the position of largest hospitality company in the world with over 1.5 million listings in over 34,000 cities in 192 countries, all within the space of seven years! Some advice from this quester supremo: "Next time you have a crazy idea and it gets rejected, I want you to think about this." Something to reflect on because as I demonstrate in this book, Chesky's quest to dominate the hotel industry fits neatly with the three qualities of a quest: the idea appeared crazily impossible; it delivers meaningful benefits to millions of travellers; and, the quest's target destination was always clear. But for now back to horology.

Büsser did not come from a family with money and after graduating with a Master's degree in micro-technology engineering, his first job was with the luxury watch manufacturer Jaeger-LeCoultre. Rising swiftly through the ranks of middle and senior management in 1998, at the age of 31 he was snapped up by venerable jewellery house Harry Wilson to head up their rare timepiece division. Over a seven-year period until 2005 when he departed, Büsser grew the business from seven employees to 80 and had increased revenue by 1,000 percent to $80 million. In the process he contributed to the legacy of a top-flight brand, which was later acquired by the Swatch Group for one-billion dollars in 2013. Büsser had soared to the height of his profession: "I had all that men typically want — power, recognition, money — and couldn't have been less happy," he says.

So why risk it all? Why invest near a million dollars of his own money, move into a small flat, live like a student and sacrifice two years of salary? Two reasons: firstly, Büsser's contract was up for renewal with Harry Wilson and the company's lawyers wanted to include a new non-compete clause should he ever leave. He had no intention of resigning from Harry Wilson, knowing he needed near tenfold the capital he had available to start a watch company, but he did not want to have a corporation controlling his life. But the second reason was more compelling, Büsser had the belief and the obsession to follow his quest, which in his own words is to: "Design and craft each year a radical and original horological masterpiece."

In the end his quest paid off and, "finally in June 2007 at the very last moment, when there was no money left, none of my personal money, none of the money of the company, we managed to deliver the first two pieces."

4.

John Harrison was an unlikely quester who took on the establishment and beat the prevailing wisdom of the day. Like Büsser, he was also on a quest to achieve the impossible by creating unique timepieces. Born in 1693 in Foulby, near Barrow-on-Humber in North Lincolnshire, into a family of carpenters, Harrison became aware of the longitude reward in 1726 and set out on a quest that would dominate the rest of his life. His quest to crack the longitude code meant that against all odds he developed not one but five workable solutions. These timepieces have become the most fêted and significant timekeeping devices ever constructed. Harrison's quest resulted in innovations that have saved thousands of lives and which, according to Martin Rees, Astronomer Royal and chair of the current day Longitude Committee, had: "An enormous impact on the world – on communication, commerce, travel, medicine and far wider ranging areas of global society."

Any clockmaker hoping his sea-clock would win the £20,000 prize on offer from the Act of Parliament was in for an uphill battle. To win the prize, an inventor would firstly have to convince the establishment – which was biased towards a lunar solution – that his timepiece was even worth testing. Isaac Newton was chair of the Board of Longitude and as president of the Royal Society resolutely insisted that astronomy held the only viable solution telling one obtuse enquirer: "I've told you oftener than once that it is not to be found by clock work...nothing but Astronomy is sufficient."

Secondly, they would need to find a solution that was accurate within 60 miles of hitting its mark. Let's put this into perspective: Jonathon Betts says in *Time Restored*: "If the longitude solution was to be by timekeeper, then the timekeeping required to achieve this goal would have to be within 2.8 seconds a day, a performance considered impossible for any clock at sea and unthinkable for a watch, even under the very best conditions."

John Harrison was the 18th century counterpart of Steve Jobs. Like the modern-day business icon, Harrison was a change agent, the leading architect and designer masterminding an emerging disruptive technology, which would transform the face of the world during his era. Like Jobs, Harrison was fastidious about design and not easily shifted from his viewpoint and opinions on how things should work. His tenacity, obsessive belief and skills meant he was able to craft the most significant clocks in world history. The antiquarian William Stukeley wrote of Harrison's timepieces: "The sweetness of the motion cannot be sufficiently admired." Harrison's timepieces, which can be viewed today at Greenwich Museum in working order 300 years later, were ground breaking and their design revolutionary.

No one is sure what fuelled John Harrison's interest in horology or where he developed the skills necessary to become a master clockmaker. He learnt carpentry from his father and this may have given him an advantage as Rory McEvoy, Curator of Horology at Greenwich, explains: "Harrison came at things from a different angle, almost from first principles. He wasn't indoctrinated with current watchmaking ideas."

His first clocks were crafted almost entirely of wood and he demonstrated great levels of ingenuity and original thinking. Harrison was awarded the commission to construct a clock in Brocklesby Park Estate for the Pelham family. The clock was revolutionary, using two ingenious designs. His first innovation was an oil-free calibre. Oils available in the 18th century were derived from animal fats and were the curse of horologists, clogging bearings and causing watches to run inconsistently and even halt operations. Harrison exhibited the capability of great questers, their ability to join the dots between disparate systems in a way that disrupts the status quo. With a stroke of genius he used the tropical hardwood lignum vitae, which contains a natural lubricant, thus masterfully eliminating the need for any oil in the clock mechanisms.

His second invention was the intricate design of a near-frictionless escapement, the part of a clock that drives energy to the pendulum. Called the grasshopper escapement because of its distinctive insect-like leg action, Harrison was able to eliminate the use of animal oils and create frictionless motion. This masterpiece now nearly 300 years old still performs proudly above the stables in Brocklesby House and is a testament to Harrison's great skills and lasting legacy of finding solutions for doing the impossible.

5.

There are good reasons behind believing some things are impossible especially when they have been built into the societal or organisational psyche. Greg Satell, a *Forbes* journalist and unconventional thinker explains, "We spend a good portion of our lives learning established models. We go to school, train for a career and hone our craft. We make great efforts to learn basic principles and are praised when we show that we have grasped them. As we strive to become masters of our craft we find that our proficiency increases, so too does our success and status. A new idea, whether it be a scientific principle or an operational model, gains power through its capacity to solve problems. As it proves its worth, it gains acceptance and becomes established."

Achieving the impossible therefore requires challenging established paradigms and principles that are generally well accepted. This is not an easy task because as we learn and experience behaviours, they become hardwired in our brains through a process that neuroscientists call Hebbian plasticity. The expression "neurons that fire together wire together" is attributed to neuropsychologists Donald Hebb and Carla Shantz. The phrase essentially explains the chemical reaction going on in our brains as we learn.

Over time, specific neurons become associated with each behaviour, emotion and feeling. Alvaro Pascual-Leone another neuroscientist, gives a brilliant analogy in the book, *The Brain That Changes Itself*, in which he compared the brain to a snowy hill in winter: "When we first go down a hill in a sled, we can be flexible because we have the option of taking various paths through the soft snow each time. If we begin to favour certain paths they become speedy and efficient, guiding the sled swiftly down the hill. Changing these paths becomes increasingly difficult, as we literally become stuck in the ruts that we have created." Human behaviour and thoughts operate on the same principle. Our behaviour creates preferred chemical pathways in our brains that eventually make these behaviours so efficient that they are difficult to change, we become "stuck in a rut".

As we learn a particular way of doing things in our organisation, profession or industry, it becomes accepted "best practice", which, in turn, is hardwired in our brain as the correct way to do things. We are encouraged, rewarded and controlled into complying and conforming with accepted best practice and to deviate from these accepted paradigms actually violates and offends our intellectual sense of how the world works.

Hebb's Law, which has since been proven, states that learning is not simply something impressed upon a passive brain, but a process in which the cellular structure of the brain is permanently modified. The difficulty, therefore, in going against the grain to prove the impossible possible, is that the resulting behaviour threatens to upset the applecart of accepted wisdom and places in question the validity of the paradigms that have given power and prominence to the establishment. Hence, people on quests get a lot of pushback. The reason why few people or organisations embark on quests, is that they are hard strategies that involved breaking down and unlearning established paradigms and then rewiring the brain to change behaviours. Essentially when you embark on an organisational quest you need to rewire the way parts of your organisation thinks! But as Mark Twain said, "It ain't what you don't know that gets you into trouble. It's what you know for sure that just ain't so."

Organisational models work in much the same way. In 1975, Steven Sasson invented the digital camera. Kodak was his employer at the time, however, his bosses who clearly felt the new paradigm offended their senses of the world, told him that that camera would never see the light of day. Sasson believed that two million pixels would be capable of competing against 110 negative film. His first digital camera produced only ten thousand pixels so the quality was not great. Executives asked when digital would compete against film, so using Moore's Law, which predicts how fast computing technology advances, he estimated 15 to 20 years. "When you're talking to a bunch of corporate guys about 18 to 20 years in the future, when none of those guys will still be in the company, they don't get too excited about it," said Sasson in an interview with the *New York Times*. Unable to shift with digital photography Kodak filed for bankruptcy in 2012.

In a world of disruptive change, embarking on quests as a core strategy is imperative for success and competitive advantage because: firstly, the rewards are massive when you are at the forefront of creating a new paradigm; and secondly, if you do not, you will be disrupted by someone else who figures out how to make the impossible possible. We've already explored this with Chesky's Airbnb, which took under a decade to disrupt the hotel industry. Uber, the transportation company, started by Travis Kalanick disrupted the taxi industry worldwide in five years. The trend where questers reshape the industrial landscape is not an aberration that will go back to normal, it is now the normal.

It's important to reflect that current paradigms were once radical thinking too; it is an evolutionary, sometimes a revolutionary process. Sir Isaac Newton, the same person Harrison came up against in his longitude quest, was considered a radical thinker who reshaped the laws of nature and ushered in new era mechanics, until, that is, Einstein created a new paradigm of relativity by showing that Newton's mechanics were flawed.

During the Age of Quests the speed at which businesses and industries are being disrupted is increasing. The world is changing and moving too quickly to stick with trusted old paradigms. The only way to keep up with the pace of change is to identify the quests in your world of influence that will have a meaningful difference. Constant adaption is the only viable strategy and people on quests are capable of adapting because they understand the importance and the value in shifting paradigms. A quest by its very nature is worth making the necessary sacrifices to rewire behaviour because people become passionate about the meaningful difference the quest will deliver.

This is why Büsser was prepared to sacrifice so much to achieve his quest. Indeed some questers become even more passionate and fired up when they are told their quest is impossible or crazy. "When Harrison said watches were the solution everyone thought he had finally gone mad, because everyone knew [the prevailing wisdom and paradigm of the day] that watches were useless," says Jonathan Betts, an expert on Harrison's watches. But Harrison proved that his technology and designs did indeed provide the solution for the longitude problem.

6.

Over 40 years Harrison crafted five marine timepieces, each watch named chronologically from H1 to H5. These stretched the boundaries of watchmaking and were pieces of design mastery and artwork in their own right. The key to Harrison's success as a quester was his ingenuity value coupled with an ability to reimagine even his own inventions.

In his quest to make timepieces that were: impervious to the motion of waves, could perform as well in the freezing temperatures of the Antarctic circles, as it would in the searing heat in the tropics, Harrison invented numerous world firsts.

The journey of a quest requires questers to be innovative and dream up craft-creative solutions. Questers do not have the benefit of previous experience, in most instances no one has ever been there before. Being on a quest involves covering unchartered terrain. What worked before is no longer a guarantee for success. Leaders on a quest continually have to unlearn and relearn. In his horology quest Harrison's creatively developed two major innovations still used today. The first was a bimetallic strip for thermostats of all kinds, and, secondly, to aid frictionless motion, he invented encased ball-bearings that are found in most modern-day machinery. To achieve the impossible, world-first inventions are often required and in the case of Harrison's quest, the benefits to society are still here 300 years later.

Agility and adaptability are important hallmarks of great questers, that ability to rethink and relearn how things work. In watch H4 Harrison performed a complete 180-degree turn and came up with the winning timepiece. Rather than going bigger he went small, minute in fact, compared to his previous watches. Harrison shrunk his original design of large sea-clocks to a design the size of a pocket watch.

This switch in direction was as sudden and a great a change as an oil tanker doing a hand-break turn but it worked. Rather than being wedded to the direction he had taken in developing his first three monstrous models, Harrison was able to execute an about-turn, unlearn and relearn in order to engineer the winning technology. By shrinking the timepiece Harrison had to jettison his pendant system that had served him so well in his earlier clocks and come up with an entirely new format. His invention was not only beautiful in design but genius in execution. To overcome the motion of waves, Harrison created a watch that oscillates five times per second – too fast for even the biggest wave to jostle.

To win the longitude reward, any submission to the board had to be subjected to numerous tests and meet the criteria laid down by the Act of Longitude. Harrison found himself not only having to overcome the greatest scientific and engineering challenges of his era but also having to fight against the establishment and an old guard protecting its own entrenched interests. Harrison was living proof that grit, determination and adaptability are needed more than talent to get ahead in life. The Board of Longitude was continuously shifting the goalposts creating new rules and criteria for the reward. Rivals like Neville Maskelyne, the Astronomer Royal and a member of the Board of Longitude, criticised Harrison's work and publicly undermined him. Pushing against the tide of resistance from naysayers requires questers to demonstrate great degrees of resilience, self-belief and a strong sense of purpose. Unsurprisingly, towards the end of his relationship with the board, Harrison believed there was a conspiracy preventing him from winning the prize. He was 79 years old, and had dedicated his life to the longitude quest. In desperation he made an appeal to the highest authority and was summoned for an interview with King George III who is said to have remarked, "You have been cruelly treated...by God, [Harrison] I will see you righted!"

Harrison's H5 timepiece was put on trial by the king and performed superbly. For this he was finally recognised for solving the longitude problem. In total, Harrison received £23,065 for his quest. He received £4,315 in increments from the Board of Longitude for his work, £10,000 as an interim payment for H4 in 1765 and £8,750 from Parliament in 1773.

Throughout his quest, Harrison revealed his immense talent as a quester. He was a tenacious visionary with steadfast belief in his ability to re-engineer watch technology to solve the greatest quest of his century. When required, he was agile and adaptive enough to completely rethink designs, overcoming a stuck-in-a-rut mentality. Nor did he fear failure, preferring to unlearn and relearn. Like Steve Jobs did not invent digital music or smartphones, Harrison did not invent the timepiece but both these questers took the nascent technology of their day to a higher level.

In July 1775, Captain Cook, returned from his voyage of discovery having used a copy of H4 – the original deemed by the Admiralty to be too valuable itself to be sent on the voyage. After a voyage of three years, sailing from the Tropics to the Antarctic the watch performed admirably never exceeding eight seconds during the entire voyage. Cook referred to the watch as "our faithful guide through all the vicissitudes of climates."

Almost one year after Cook's return, on the day of his 83rd birthday, 24 March 1776, John Harrison passed away at his house on Red Lion Square, London. He'd lived to see his quest fulfilled.

Chapter Six

Making The Impossible Possible

*"I have always believed that creativity makes the impossible possible and
is understandable and relatable to every person in the world"*
Paul Cummins

1.

Not everyone steps out on grand world-changing quests. But
everybody can embark on quests that improve "their immediate
world", the part of their community where they have the greatest
influence. We all have a sphere of influence; Stephen Covey in his
immensely successful book the *Seven Habits of Highly Successful People*
references the "circle of concern" and the "circle of influence". You can
be concerned about global poverty but your circle of influence may be
limited. That doesn't mean you shouldn't go on a quest to make a
meaningful difference. Every year Graeme Codrington, one of my
partners at TomorrowToday Global, embarks on a quest to "Live
Below the Line". This challenge involves choosing to eat and drink on
only £1 a day for a gruelling five days. Doing this enables him to raise
funds and awareness. Together a community of over 4,000 questers
living in the UK, who are passionate about ending poverty, have raised
£700,000 to empower some of the world's poorest communities.
Graeme said to me that he doesn't have the ability to end poverty but
through his circle of influence he can make a difference. Quests can
therefore be big or small, personal or professional but the fundamental
framework remains the same.

The reality is anyone can be a quester. With this in mind how does a
13-year-old Berkshire boy, the age of the youngest British soldier at
the Battle of the Somme, have any connection with an unknown 39-

year-old English artist from Derbyshire who embarked on a quest that captivated the world?

The answer lies in a quest conceived by ceramicist Paul Cummins: to create a sea of 888,246 ceramic poppies to be displayed at the Tower of London to commemorate British and colonial deaths from World War One.

This "Blood Swept Lands and Seas of Red installation" was inspired by the last will and testament of a Derbyshire trooper who joined up in the earliest days of the war and died in Flanders. Contained in this document found among other old records in the Chesterfield Public Office were the lines from a poem: "The blood-swept lands and seas of red, where angels fear to tread", which evoked an almost visceral reaction in Cummins. He explained that, being dyslexic, he saw things in a different way from other people. As he put it: "to see the actual note brought back memories of red". Though Cummins had no idea of the person's name or where he was buried, the soldier's meaning was clear: everyone he knew was dead around him and the lands were awash with people's blood.

The Blood Swept Lands and Seas of Red
By Anon – Unknown Soldier

The blood swept lands and seas of red,
Where angels dare to tread.
As I put my hand to reach,
As God cried a tear of pain as the angels fell,
Again and again.

As the tears of mine fell to the ground
To sleep with the flowers of red
As any be dead

My children see and work through fields of my
Own with corn and wheat,

Blessed by love so far from pain of my resting
Fields so far from my love.

It be time to put my hand up and end this pain
Of living hell, to see the people around me
Fall someone angel as the mist falls around
And the rain so thick with black thunder I hear
Over the clouds, to sleep forever and kiss
The flower of my people gone before time
To sleep and cry no more

I put my hand up and see the land of red,
This is my time to go over,
I may not come back
So sleep, kiss the boys for me

From this beautiful poem came the inspiration for Paul Cummins's idea of designing an individual poppy for every British or Commonwealth soldier who had been killed in the front lines during the Great War. The number also included people who died after the war as a result of wounds received during battle. Said Cummins, "I wanted every flower to be individual, each one representing a soldier. They couldn't be made in any other way or in any other country. They had to be British. We used traditional techniques to reflect how things would have been made during the war."

And now that the idea had been conceived, it needed more than just one visionary to make it happen. Traditional techniques naturally implied that each and every poppy would be handmade: "I prefer to make my work how it used to be made 100 or 150 years ago, which is with as little machinery as possible." Explaining his thought process, Cummins stated, "People should get involved in physically making something, so that it means something more." He also spoke about creativity and what it means: "Ever since I was a young boy, moulding, sculpture and creation has been a focal point for me. I have always believed that creativity makes the impossible possible and is understandable and relatable to every person in the world."

With an incredibly tight timeline of just six months to fabricate hundreds of thousands of poppies before the exhibition was unveiled at the Tower of London on 5 August, Cummins was going to need assistance. "I normally make everything myself. On a scale like this, I can't. I need help," Cummins explained during the production period. In February 2014, work began in his studio – Paul Cummins Ceramics Ltd in Pride Park, Derby. Although perhaps Cummins might not have seen this project as a quest, it immediately began to fulfil two crucial element of a quest: it was a deeply heartfelt, emotional commitment to achieving an outcome for oneself and the greater good. And, the production of 888,246 handmade ceramic poppies in such a short space of time was seemingly impossible.

The greater good is indeed what captured people's imaginations, encouraging them to join his quest. One artist, Lorraine Clewlow, summed it up very well. "When I was first told about it, my own artwork is about memories, it rang a chord in my psyche; it resonated well with me." Like any true quest, Cummins's project was inspirational and it offered people a sense of purpose, a True North and a way to recognise those people who had lost their lives a century before. The centenary was indeed a most poignant moment to think back. Said Cummins at the time, "It looks like it's going to be the biggest World War One celebration this year," he said. "Most of the companies in Derby, certainly in Pride Park, have helped out in some way." This was another important aspect of the greater good – Cummins also saw his masterpiece as an opportunity to put Derby back on the map. Derby had once been the cradle of the Industrial Revolution; the waters of its 66-mile river Derwent powered the first industrial-scale cotton mills invented by Richard Arckwright the founding father of this remarkable era.

With this inspiration behind it, the work on the poppies progressed with surprising speed and the project began to create its own momentum. Cummins said, "Surprisingly enough I've managed to gather a lot of people who – seventy percent are artists – but they all have a direct link to a member in the Armed Forces or people they know have died."

One of the 35 artists at work interviewed for a Royal Palace's promotional piece on the poppies, explained, "We're all focused on what the project is about." This overall focus on one soul, one perfect and unique poppy seemed almost overwhelming. Its foundation is, of course, a sense of empathy and connection with those who fell. This quest grew and became bigger than Cummins, the individual. People embarking on this project were both inspired and empowered by their own participation in it.

"When we started making them and they started appearing, piles and piles of poppies just growing and being stacked up, was absolutely incredible to see," said Clewlow. "In World War One – these young lads didn't have much training so they were as fragile as clay and they were cut down like flowers in the early stages of bloom," she continued, "so the symbolism isn't lost on us, far from it." Another fellow quester added, "We're all immensely pleased to be doing what we're doing and now that we've seen the installation open it's altered our whole perception – it's made us all want to give more and work even harder."

The workload to meet Cummins's deadline was intense – a 23-hour-a-day split between a staff of 52 people working three overlapping shifts, just to get the quantity of poppies required out. In total, they were making 7,000 flowers a day in order to meet the daunting six-figure target. And not every poppy passed Cummins's quality test. "I'm quite paranoid about them looking how I want them to look within reason, and if they don't I won't let them go out." The sheer scale of the production was astounding, with each artist producing between 800 to 1,000 poppies a day.

The basic process for producing the poppies was this. Blocks of clay were sliced and made into sheets. Large and small flower-head shapes were stamped out and placed together, with a circle cut out the middle. Each artist would arrange the petals to look more like flowers, and then they were fired in the kiln. After being glazed, corks would be inserted and the wire stalks – some as tall as two feet, would be added by volunteers at the Tower of London.

Quests are never achieved without setbacks, dedication and sacrifice. Just months after embarking on his adventure, in May 2014, Cummins lost the middle finger of his right hand during an accident with an industrial clay roller. "I did nearly kill myself halfway through. We had to rally the troops. Morphine helped," said Cummins. He could no longer make any poppies himself because of his injury. Yet despite this, he had the resources and support of a committed team to continue on his quest while their leader was down.

But making the poppies was only one element of the quest. For the poppies to have the kind of visual impact Cummins envisioned, he had to stir up and engage the passion of stage designer Tom Piper. "This could end up being epic," said Piper in a blog written after "Paul came to the Tower with the idea to fill the moat with poppies".

Piper, who along with assistant Lily Arnold had worked with the prestigious Royal Shakespeare Company – quests always attract the best talent – joined Cummins's quest to help design the poignant installation. "Our role is to work out how to place these around the moat... In terms of pure logistics, we worked out that it would take one person three-and-a-half years to install all the poppies," said Piper.

Their artwork filled 16 acres of moats surrounding the Tower of London, creating a scarlet sea of remembrance, which would act as a focal point for mourning a great and tragic loss. There was also going to be a cascade or "Weeping Window" section where Piper would arrange the poppies so they appeared to pour out of an opening in one of the turrets. A wave of flowers would also wash over the causeway used by visitors to enter the castle. Said Piper in an interview with

Dezeen: "They could be tears, they could be blood flowing or it could be poppies growing unnaturally tall to climb over the walls."

Yeoman Warder Jim Duncan described what came next as a "major logistical exercise" – planting the poppies at the Tower of London. An army of volunteers would from the first day keep adding to the sea of poppies for a period of three months, with the last flower due to be planted, symbolically, on November 11. Each day of the poppy planting an average of 200 volunteers arrived at nine to help. The shift would last four hours and the process was a little more complex than simply hammering a spike in the ground. Before that, the ground to be planted would have been prepared from five in the morning. The volunteers would be split into groups of 40 to 50 people, and be instructed on how to put the six component parts of the poppies together at a logistical briefing where DVDs were shown. The teams were then broken into even smaller groups – some planting, some inserting the rods and various other jobs, which they would all have a chance to perform. On some days as many as 5,000 poppies were planted in a shift!

Paul Cummins commented on the sense of unity regarding the project. "It's overwhelming that they have wanted to do it on this scale and there are thousands of people doing it." In total some 16,000 volunteers planted the poppies and 11,000 people volunteered to take them out, clean them and assist with posting them. Many reported the "sense of privilege" in being involved, and even an "eerie feeling" knowing that when they planted the poppy, it represented a real soldier, a lost soul.

The fact that so many people were prepared to give up their free time for this quest is a key element. As Cummins put it, "We always hoped the installation would capture the public imagination yet we could not predict the level of support we have received and for this we are truly grateful. I think they have taken ownership of it and the reason why I think they have done that is that specific number, 888,246 – not a random number – that is the number of British and Colonial soldiers who lost their lives in the First World War." Lt Tim Montagu, a member of the current British Armed Forces put it more succinctly, explaining the poppy planting as a chance to "forge links with family who fought and died in the Great War".

Deborah Shaw, Head of Creative Programming for the Royal Palaces, mentioned also that open installations, like the one Cummins conceived, offer lots of opportunities to get involved. She added that this one in particular was the most "animated evolving artwork". One specific example of this was that people were able, via their website, to nominate people whose names they believed should be read out at a special ceremony at the Tower every evening. After the names of 180 people were read out, the ceremony was concluded by a lone bugler calling the last post – a truly evocative and mournful reminder. This offered her, she felt, her "own personal moment of reflection".

Viewed by an estimated five million people in person, the sight of the ceramic poppies cascading out of the Tower also became one of the most iconic images of 2014, and for a time was the most viewed photograph on Google. Perhaps there was something about the temporary nature of the installation that also made it more appealing, even whimsical. Onlookers felt they were witnessing something great: "It just affects me deeply, it really does," said one man. Other people interviewed spoke about having to see the piece in person, or feeling that they would regret it later.

Cummins, however, was happy that the exhibition was going to come to an end, as he said its temporary existence reflected our brief time on Earth. "The idea was it will only be there for a finite time like we are," he said. "It will be nice to keep it here but it isn't mine anymore—it belongs to the world now." This too is an important part of a quest; it can no longer belong just to the person who first embarks upon it, but those who join it as well.

Agnes Atkinson, who moved to the UK from the Philippines 22 years before was one of these people. She was chosen to assist with the poppy removal. "I think I am so lucky to be picked and be here for the first morning," she said. "To be part of it is such an amazing experience." And like any quest, this one was not without added effort – even as the installation was being dismantled: "Some of the poppies are really quite stubborn, so you really have to dig your hands down and pull it."

Another element of the quest is that it encourages innovation, and the memorial certainly fits this category. Cummins described the method of funding and creation as being "revolutionary" – not only did the public come on board in terms of labour, but also by buying all of the ceramic poppies used in the installation for £25. Ten percent of the sale price was divided between six military service charities: Cobeso, Combat Stress, Coming Home, Help for Heroes, The Royal British Legion and SSAFA. A total of £9 million was raised in the process. Private investors who helped fund the project were also expected to benefit.

But this brings us back to my question of the link between Cummins and the 13-year-old Berkshire boy at the beginning of this chapter. Together, they represent a full circle, as on Armistice Day – November 11 – during a two-minute silence, the boy, called Cadet Harry Hayes planted the 888,246th and final poppy in the Tower of London's moat. This, in honour of his great-great uncle, Private Patrick Kelly of 1st Battalion The Irish Guards, who was killed in action on September 27, 1918, just weeks before the war's end.

Paul said he was inundated with people wanting to play their part in creating the sea of poppies. "What has really blown me away has been the people who have volunteered to actually put the poppies into the ground," he said. "There are people from Hong Kong, the States, even Vietnam. It's a little bit crazy. It's not my work anymore, it's everybody's." That is the power of a quest the impossible becomes possible.

The passion and empathy of Cummins's quest evoked such emotional fervour that what was started as a memorial, became more of a phenomenon. And while the Blood Swept Lands and Seas of Red may have started as a quest to commemorate death, it took on a life of its own.

Part Three

The Power of a
Target Destination

"Humanity is on a journey to something far beyond anything we can even comprehend today."
James Martin

Chapter Seven

Adventurous Journeys

"Men wanted for hazardous journey to the south pole. Small wages, bitter cold, long months of complete darkness, constant danger. Safe return doubtful. Honour and recognition in case of success."
Sir Ernest Shackleton

1.

This quote comes from the legendary advert the great leader and adventurer Sir Ernest Shackleton is believed to have posted when seeking fellow questers to join him on his Antarctic quests. In speaking of it afterward he said, "So overwhelming was the response to his appeal that it seemed as though all the men of Great Britain were determined to accompany him."

The crazier and bolder the idea, often the greater is the attraction. There is a lovely anecdote of a NASA janitor from around the time of the Apollo 11 moon landing who was cleaning the computer room at mission control. When a reporter stopped to ask him what he was doing, the janitor replied, "I'm helping to put a man on the moon." It is not only astronauts and adventurers who get to go on quests. There is a role for anyone who dares to venture out and find new ground. Quests offer meaning to our lives and people want to be involved, no matter how big or small a part they play in its success.

Quests are part of the human spirit that keeps humanity driving forward. We see evidence of these commitments throughout this book. In the case of Paul Cummins, thousands of volunteers joined his quest and gave freely of their time and energy to make the *"Blood Swept Lands and Seas of Red"* poppies installation the success it was.

Like Shackleton, leaders of quests discover that the power of the quest means there is seldom a shortage of talented applicants, especially when the destination the questers are going towards is crystal clear. When asked why she left a promising career in New York to join Maximilian Büsser, the CEO of MB&F, Eléonor Picciotto a talented and highly sought-after PR professional responded by saying, "For the adventure so-to-speak! There had to be a good reason for me to leave the city that never sleeps that is New York City, to move to the grand village that is Geneva. If it wasn't for one of Max's new crazy ideas – the destination – there is a high probability that I would have never taken that jump."

Eric Giroud, a watch designer considered by his peers to be one of the most exciting talents in the world of horology, says he joined the MB&F quest because, "when Max first shared his new project idea with me, I thought he was mad. Now, as I consider creative madness one of the most appealing illnesses, of which I suffer also, I immediately accepted to be part of this extraordinary adventure." Through his quest Maximillian Büsser has been able to attract an A-Team of questers, "friends" as he calls them – it's what the "F" in MB&F stands for. Friends are "talented individuals, harnessing their passion and creativity and crediting each individual's essential role, MB&F uses their synergy to become much greater than the sum of its parts. MB&F is above all a human adventure, with just one quest: to create incredible horological machines."

Virginie Meylan who heads up trade marketing at MB&F says "the philosophy was a great motivation for me to join MB&F. Everybody has dreams but never dares to follow or realise them... I wanted to be part of the team and participate in the realisation of these amazing machines." Together the team of questing friends at MB&F are pushing the limits of horology and journeying towards a destination that creates a totally different dimensional experience.

2.

According to Sebastian Thrun, introduced earlier in this book, there are many different ways to climb a mountain. He says, "Execution to me is all about the way you would climb a mountain you've never climbed before. If you waver along the way, if you debate, if you become uncertain about the objective, then you're not going to make it. It's important that you keep climbing. And it's important that you acknowledge that you don't have all the answers. So you will make mistakes, and you will have to back up, learn, and improve. But you should not change your goal." The quest, the final destination on an adventurous journey does not change.

In *The Lord of the Rings,* Frodo's Baggins, the central character in J.R.R. Tolkien's legendarium is on a quest to destroy the One Ring in the fires of Mount Doom. He undergoes setback after setback and is forced to adapt his plans and strategies. Remaining agile, resilient and persevering becomes essential to fulfilling the quest. Frodo has to experiment, take risks and unlearn. But throughout the trials and tribulations the quest's goal, the final destination – the centre of Mordor, where Frodo hurled the One Ring into the molten fires – that destination never changes.

The destination defines the quest and influences how its journey takes shape. The destination becomes the sole reason for embarking and starting on a quest. But without a clear, objective and outcome-focused destination a quest becomes meaningless. A destination, therefore, needs to be described as an outcome and not an activity. A quest offers a clearly identifiable outcome or in Thrun's words a "mountain" to climb.

The best quests are always conveyed as an outcome. For Maximilian Büsser, the quest is to "to design and craft each year a radical and original horological masterpiece." Each year a truly original and amazing piece of horology has been crafted and as the website says, "in 2015 MB&F celebrates its 10th Anniversary: 10 years and 10 calibres!"

For Professor Steven Cowley, his quest and those of his peers at ITER and JET is for a sustained fusion burn. Paul Cummins's quest had a crystal-clear outcome: to handcraft and plant 888,246 ceramic poppies in the moat at the Tower of London by 11 November 2014. For US President Kennedy, the quest was to "go to the moon in this decade".

For Steve Jobs, the quest was to "launch a great computer in a book". "The Future Isn't What It Used To Be" was the theme of the 1983 International Design Conference in Aspen where Steve Jobs, the great computer pioneer, gave one of his very first public talks. A recording of his talk languished in a box undiscovered until John Celuch, an attendee at the small conference, found it after Jobs had passed away. The unique and rare recording provides new insight into Jobs and helps us understand the great lengths he went to achieving his quest. On the tape recording Jobs is heard saying, *"Apple's strategy is really simple. What we want to do is put an incredibly great computer in a book that you can carry around with you and learn how to use in twenty minutes and we want to do it this decade."*

We can test Job's ideal to check if it observes the three qualities of a quest. Back in 1983 the idea that a computer could be the size of a book would have been considered crazily impossible, thus meeting the first criterion. In the early 1980s computers were still massive, especially by today's standards. A fully functioning computer that you could have carried around and learn to use in twenty minutes! Crazy! Send for the men with the white coats! Accomplishing his quest would benefit millions of people, even change the world, meeting the second questing quality. And, the third quality, a clear target destination, well, "an incredibly great computer in a book" offered a clear and targeted destination for questers at Apple.

Quests often involve setbacks that require rerouting, and here is the reason why a targeted destination is such a crucial questing quality. It wasn't until 3 April 2010, 27 years after Jobs announced his "quest" that he revealed the "magical iPad". During the intervening time he was banished from Apple and fired as their CEO. He spent years "exiled" to the computer wastelands of Next Computers and ultimately navigated his way back to Apple via a life-defining adventure with Pixar and Disney. The tenacity, agility and resilience of Steve Jobs is well documented but it is interesting to observe that he never lost sight of his ultimate quest – launching a great computer in a book. Without a targeted destination, the journey becomes objectiveless and meandering, something many businesses and leaders who are not on quests fall victim to. Jobs knew his destination and regardless of the obstacles that were thrown in front of him he merely rerouted and stayed true to reaching his final destination.

Jobs may not have articulated his strategy as a quest but it had all of the three important qualities of one. The parallels with Jobs, the founders at Third Rock Ventures, Büsser and other questers in this book are striking. Over their journeys they had to adjust and adapt their strategies but they stayed true to their ultimate destination, their True North, their quest.

Because the quest offers a destination, it is easy to communicate and once people know the destination they are free to engage and contribute, to play their own part. They no longer need managers to tell them what to do; they become inspired and motivated to get on and just do it.

Once a quest has taken off, those who take up and heed the call of the quest also own it. Organisations employ very bright people but research shows disturbingly low levels of engagement because employees are seldom treated as capable adults. Organisations prefer to manage and monitor people to the nth degree rather than to set their talent free on quests that may change the world and deliver competitive advantages. Organisations and managers do this because of the industrial mindset of control, conformity and compliance. We've been taught to believe that work without management is chaos, too risky to contemplate, but it is surprising how efficient self-organising systems become when the destination is understood and the quest is meaningful.

Chapter Eight

The Greatest Quest in Sports History

"The most important things in the world exist only in our imagination."
Yuval Noah Harari

1.

The America's Cup is the world's most prestigious sailing event. It is a contest between two yachts, *the Challenger* and *the Defender* who compete to win what is considered the oldest international sporting trophy, a baroque sterling silver ewer affectionately known as "Auld Mug". Over the duration of its 164-year history, the event has attracted the world's greatest sailors, tested the prowess of the very best boat and sail designers and challenged the proficiencies of experienced management and fundraising teams who support each team's endeavour to lift victoriously the legendary cup.

The event has a rich and complex history dating back to 1851. The Royal Yacht Squadron hosted the inaugural event raced in the English Channel around the Isle of Wight. As the schooner *America* approached the finishing line in first place, Queen Victoria reputedly asked, "Who is coming second?" The famous apocryphal answer was, "Ah, Your Majesty, there is no second". The Cup was subsequently renamed the "America's Cup", after the name of the winning schooner and donated to its owners the New York Yacht Club, on the condition it be made "available for perpetual international competition".

As there are only two competitors in the America's Cup there can only be "the winner" and "the loser". The quest for both teams is a straightforward affair – *to win Auld Mug* and this translates simply into winning more races than the competing yacht over the duration of the regatta.

The Cup's governance stipulates that the Defender sets the rules under which the next regatta will be raced. This allows the Defender to decide the yacht design, number of races and even where the event will be held. These "home-field advantages" mean the outcome is traditionally a one-sided affair. In its long history, all teams bar one have successfully defended The Cup at least once and most defended it successfully several times. Historical trends therefore suggest the Defender has a 33:1 chance of retaining The Cup for at least one challenge.

Oracle Team USA won the 33rd America's Cup, it was their first win in three attempts and the 34th America's Cup represented their first defence. Backed by business magnate Larry Ellison, the then fifth wealthiest man in the world and founder of global computer technology giant Oracle. Ellison once said, "The biggest lie told in professional sports is, we're just going out there to have fun." Ellison wanted to win in everything he did and coming second was never an option. He had built a business empire off the back of being controlling, demanding conformity and enforcing compliance. When asked by *CBS News* anchor Charlie Rose why he had to win the America's Cup yacht race Ellison replied, "It's funny, because I realized after losing twice that my personality wouldn't allow me to quit while losing. And then after winning the America's Cup, I discovered my personality doesn't allow me to quit while winning! I don't smoke, but I do sail."

As the Defender, Ellison now had history on his side and an abundance of financial and technological resources. Come race day, the crew of Oracle Team USA had every conceivable advantage they could have wished for. They had home-ground advantage; Ellison chose his backyard San Francisco stating, the "bay is the most spectacular natural amphitheatre for sailing". Its scenic backdrop including Golden Gate Bridge, Alcatraz and the Marina Bay waterfront offered a picture-perfect gladiatorial arena for television. That they had the lighter, more aerodynamic sailboat along with unparalleled access to performance data, technology and an unlimited budget meant the team of professional sailors were the superstars of sailing. Speculation going into the regatta was for a landslide victory with Ellison's big-money sailing machine romping away. Yet it wasn't long before Oracle Team USA was facing down the barrel of a gun, 8–1 down in a first-to-reach-nine race regatta.

How had things gone so badly wrong for Oracle Team USA that they were failing in their goal to retain Auld Mug? They clearly had the advantage on paper. Was this a case of the "tortoise" in the form of the publically funded challenger Emirates Team New Zealand steadily overtaking the complacent, arrogant and sleeping-on-the-job "hare" in the form of Oracle Team USA?

The answer to the latter question is a surprising "no". In what has been dubbed "one of the greatest comebacks in sports history", Oracle Team USA won. The improbable, implausible and even the impossible happened – all attributes of a great quest. "We weren't expecting to lose 9–8, that's for sure," said Emirates Team New Zealand boss Grant Dalton.

In respect to the former question, two things happened. Firstly, the sailors discovered an inspirational quest that they all believed in and could rally behind. Secondly, this is a human story where the passion, desire, tenacity and belief needed to achieve a quest outshone the efficiency and effectiveness of the technology and management on show. This is a story where the "hare" was released from being held back and, when fully engaged, won the race.

Using the qualities of a quest: impossible, meaningful benefits and target destination, Team Oracle USA, I would argue, was not on a quest when they first set out to win the 34th America's Cup. Winning Auld Mug was a goal, it was their mission; this is a subtle but important distinction. The team had already won The Cup; no one thought its defence was impossible, most inside and outside Oracle indeed believed it probable. They also knew historically the odds significantly favoured the Defender. Computer simulations concluded Oracle Team

USA could enter the regatta with confidence having the fastest boat ever to compete for The Cup. There is no doubt that the pressure to win was as considerable as it would be in any professional sporting event, but win was something the sailors and their management *expected* to do. They had entered the race complacent and over-confident.

But at 8–1 down, they faced an inevitable and embarrassing loss. Having believed it would be impossible for Oracle Team USA to lose, the tables had been turned and now it had become impossible for them to win. "You know what 8–1 is?" said Oracle Team skipper Jimmy Spithill to Ellison, "8–1 is motivating!" "Okay," answered Ellison, "I'll get behind that."

2.

"The most important things in the world exist only in our imagination," argues Yuval Noah Harari, an author of the best-selling book *Sapiens: A brief history of humankind*. Fiction, he says is "of immense importance, because it enabled us to imagine things collectively". Humans control the world because we are able to cooperate in large numbers and this, Harari believes, sets us apart from other species. "Human's have the ability to create new realities, fictional realities. You cannot convince a chimpanzee that if he gives you a banana he will go to chimpanzee heaven and have an endless supply of bananas," explains Harari but because humans can believe in fictional realities, leaders are able to inspire groups to achieve incredible feats.

Skipper Jimmy Spithill's "8–1 is motivational" is a fictional reality. There was no objective truth behind his fictional story, but suddenly the people at Oracle Team USA could imagine achieving a 9–8 win, something that had never been done before. The greatest comeback in sporting history was a quest they could all imagine and this inspired them. It was still going to require a lot of hard work, skill and luck, but then all quests require these.

"People come together to build a cathedral, a mosque or fight on a crusade or a jihad because they all believe in the same stories," articulates Harari in a TED talk. Humans are comfortable living with "dual realities". We have objective realities, mountains, rivers and oceans, these are examples, but they are real, they exist. But we also live with fictional realities – the belief that if we scale high mountains or sail across vast oceans we can achieve more. "Over the centuries, we have constructed on top of this objective reality a second layer of fictional reality, a reality made of fictional entities, like nations, like gods, like money, like corporations. And what is amazing is that as history unfolded, this fictional reality became more and more powerful," says Harari.

Quests form part of the human imagination that has the greatest impact. They are the pinnacles of fictional reality and the best ones stand out and inspire complete strangers to cooperate freely and change the world. This is why quests are such a potent societal and leadership force for driving change.

Oracle Team USA now had their quest's targeted destination, 9–8 clearly in their imagination. In an ironic twist of fate the team had found a "mountain" to climb; they had discovered their true quest. Their target destination was clear, unambiguous and outcome focused. Skipper Spithill used the inspiration gained from imagining a 9–8 win to help crack the code for success and win. Here is how they did it.

3.

There was a lot of speculation behind Oracle Team USA's dramatic reversal. The question everyone was asking was how, over the competition that lasted 15 days, had Oracle Team USA's speed and performance in the upwind leg improved by 60 percent from 20 to 32 knots? One theory doing the social media grapevine was that Oracle had cheated by installing a hidden computerised Stability Augmentation System, similar to those used on airplanes. This facilitated stability on the yacht and enabled the sailors to achieve the dramatically improved speeds. Inspectors measured and checked the sailboat every day and a special device was never found. Regatta Director Iain Murray even remarked on numerous instances that Oracle Team USA had been issued new certificates of compliance before "every race". The conspiracy theory remained no more than that. Another reason given was that Oracle Team USA's "sailors were rusty" having had little race match practice. This in comparison to Emirates Team NZ, which had competed in the preliminaries before becoming the official challenger and was therefore more race fit entering the finals.

Oracle Corporation's own explanation for the astounding comeback was attributed to the company's superior command of big data and cloud computing. This would be the PR line from the world's second largest information technology company. Oracle Corporation used the win to promote the "record-breaking performance of Oracle's Exadata Database Machine X3-2." They claimed their "extreme database performance machine" was the force behind winning Auld Mug. Asim Khan, Oracle's director of information technology, in an interview with the *New Zealand Herald* said, "Big data definitely helped us turn our fortunes around because without it skipper Jimmy Spithill would have just been going on intuition."

None of these theories, however, fully explains the meteoritic improvement in speed on the upwind leg that Oracle achieved in only a matter of days during the last half of the regatta. No doubt elite athletes improve as they compete together but the 11 sailors were the best money could buy. They had been training for months against a second identical sailboat skippered by none other than four-time gold medal Olympian and British champion, Ben Ainslie, who many consider the greatest living sailor. Believing they entered The Cup final so rusty to be capable of a 60 percent increase in speed within the space of a few days seems as unlikely as the conspiracy theory.

Most of Oracle Team USA's technical modifications were made early on and don't appear to have had an immediate impact on race times. Once performance improvements, however, did emerge, they happened very quickly, so much so that the rate at which Oracle Team USA caught and passed Team NZ was as dramatic as night and day. Grant Dalton, team boss at Team NZ illuminated this rapid advance in speed saying, "They got about a minute and a half faster on the beat than they were nine days ago. We were 50 seconds a beat quicker, and now they're 50 seconds quicker than us. So they've done a really amazing job to turn that around." Clearly this was not an incremental improvement; something momentous happened to release the shackles restraining Oracle Team USA.

Evidence that the Kiwis were sailing faster was visibly evident from early on with Team NZ racking up four wins in the first five races. The advantage they had was on the course's third, upwind leg, where if behind, they would easily overtake Oracle Team USA, and, if ahead, the win would be turned into an embarrassing drubbing. Since antiquity sailors have known that sailing into a headwind requires plotting a zigzag course tacking back and forth roughly at 45-degree angle to the wind in order to progress forward. Sailing upwind involves a trade-off between speed and distance covered, the greater that angle of attack into the wind, the shorter the total distance travelled but at a slower speed. Something was very wrong on the upwind leg for Oracle Team USA, "It is a shock that they've got the edge upwind," said Jimmy Spithill after losing Race 5.

Recognising that his team needed a lifeline to regroup and figure out where they were going wrong upwind, Spithill decided to use Oracle Team USA's sole postponement card after Race 5 and gained two competition-free days to fabricate a solution. Over the next 48 hours the team used the postponement to practise as well as install a set of brand-new foils developed in Ellison's R&D facility just north of Auckland. The team believed the new foils would increase speed both upwind and downwind and it was this sudden installation that gave rise to the conspiracy theory that Oracle had connected a computerised stability system illegally aiding the sailors. In addition, Ben Ainslie was drafted on board from the substitute bench as the team's tactician. Spithill and crew were now confident that the timeout, foil and crew modifications would do the trick.

The devastating answer, came quickly in Races 6 and 7, and was a resounding "no". The defeats were greater than before with Oracle Team USA losing Race 7 by a massive 66 seconds, their worst finish. Auld Mug was fast slipping away, Team NZ needed just three more wins, and they had 12 races to do it in.

After the Race 7 thrashing, Spithill, struggling with insomnia, grabbed his laptop and downloaded videos of the Kiwi team racing. He knew Oracle Team USA's vulnerability lay on the upwind leg and the biggest difference he could identify was that Emirates Team NZ were riding the foils on both the up and downwind legs.

Foiling was a technique used in competition on much smaller yachts to make them hydroplane and seemingly "fly" across water. Ellison had drafted into service Joseph Ozanne, a highly qualified data scientist and astronautical engineer and given him the task of designing "an exciting boat – something that looks like a fast and amazing machine." Having graduated from the Institut Supérieur de l'Aéronautique et de l'Espace, the prestigious French aerospace engineering school in Toulouse, Ozanne had a passion for elite sports. With experience working with teams on the Volvo Ocean Race he was considered without peer. But the task Ozanne faced to make this new super breed of America's Cup sailboats soar was immense.

This was the challenge – use a platform the size of a surfboard to support and balance, 30 feet above the water, seven tons of crew and yacht moving at over 50 mph. Ozanne faced a challenging quest just in designing a workable solution. Foiling such large boats had never been done before and most people believed it impossible, especially upwind. Ozanne, however, knew that it was a quest worth pursuing because it was from below not above the water line where the biggest gains would come. "Last Cup I was a wing designer, and then everybody believed that the wing was the key," said Ozanne just weeks before the 34th America's Cup. "But that's not true," he continued, "the most efficient way to do that is to lift the boat to reduce the volume of the floats, so you need to lift your boat out of the water. You can do that with foils, but you can't do that with the wing because it is vertical."

The foil is a single L-shaped board, found under each of the catamaran's hulls. When deployed, the foils submerge below the water line and like the wings of an aeroplane, the greater the speed, the greater the lift, until suddenly the sailboat's hulls surge free from the water. Freed from the frictional drag, a turbocharged-like acceleration catapults the sailors forward. The AC72s, the name given to the yacht used in the 34th America's Cup, look like enormous flying fish gracefully racing across the tips of waves as they sail faster than the wind. Ozanne, the design genius, had come up with a solution that not only worked but also made viewing the America's Cup a spectacular sporting sensation. "We used to consider that if a boat was gaining three meters per minute it was super quick. It's much more exciting for us now because we are dealing with massive boat speeds and speed differences. Instead of three meters per minute, we are talking about 40, 50, or 80 meters per minute," said Ozanne in an interview with the magazine *Sailing World* when talking about his new innovation.

Foiling upwind was something Spithill and crew had been unable to master. They'd tried a few times during practice runs but each time, Oracle's hulls would lurch off her foils and crash with a shudder back into the bay's cold waters.

To assist the sailors Oracle Corporation developed a software programme called the Velocity Performance Predictor. By harnessing the power of Big Data, Oracle hoped to control how their professional sailors sailed and remove the risk of sailing by intuition. Oracle wanted to win and they were confident their software and management systems gave them a controlling edge. The Velocity Performance Predictor calculated 42 degrees to be the optimal mix of speed and distance travelled when sailing upwind. Based on this information Oracle's Management decided the sailors no longer needed to use the technique of foiling when sailing upwind. Supported by the software predictions they were confident their yacht would perform faster than Emirates Team NZ upwind even without foiling. The reality was proving very different.

According to *Wall Street* journalist Stu Woo in the excellent article *Against the Wind,* "Looking at the video, Mr. Spithill could see that the Kiwis had come to a different conclusion. They were sailing at much wider angles to the wind, about 50 degrees, on average. They were covering more water but reaching higher speeds, more than enough to offset the greater distance travelled." Because it was travelling at a less aggressive angle into the wind, the sail was taking on more wind, hitting speeds high enough to rise up on the foils. Team NZ were travelling farther but at speeds that more than compensated for the extra distance. "Foiling appeared to be the key. Oracle's computers hadn't anticipated such speeds," noted Woo. Oracle's management had placed too much emphasis on their ability to use technology and systems to control the outcome and with their vast budget they had been lulled into a false sense of security.

Spithill took the discovery back to his team and according to Woo, when Ozanne recalculated the numbers, "he found the flaw in the computer model. To get going fast enough upwind to get on the foils, the yacht had to sail at an angle of between 50 to 55 degrees forcing it to cover more water, something the computer wasn't programmed to allow. In Race 8 New Zealand jumped out to an early lead. But after the boats turned upwind, Oracle was moving faster than ever. The difference was Oracle was now foiling, too." Spithill had cracked the code. Freed from the constraints the sailors were now able to focus on achieving their quest.

By initially complying and conforming to the controls and constraints placed on them by Oracle, the talented sailors were held back by the very systems and management processes that were meant to be helping them. It was not until they were freed to fully engage in their quest that the tables turned for Oracle Team USA. "With his team's prospects getting dimmer by the hour, Jimmy Spithill decided it was time to stop obeying the computers and start thinking like sailors," says Woo. Wisely and now recognising the need to unlearn his normal controlling approach, Ellison, on being told the sailors were going to sail using intuition rather than comply with what the managers and computers were telling them, responded saying, "I felt that I should keep my mouth shut and let the boats and the sailors demonstrate whether the decision was right or wrong." Ultimately his decision proved to be a wise one because rather than face a hugely embarrassing loss, Ellison and Oracle Team USA staged the greatest ever comeback in sports history.

There is no doubt that the talented sailors on board Oracle Team USA benefitted from the technology and information that was available. But the true power of the quest comes when teams and talent are able to use the power of technology to aid intuition and release their creativity rather than have rules, procedures and processes stifle and control them. As Albert Einstein said, "Computers are incredibly fast, accurate, and stupid; humans are incredibly slow, inaccurate, and brilliant; together they are powerful beyond imagination."

The dynamics that unfolded in Team Oracle USA is a story that people who work in large organisations can relate to. Each and every day this story is played out in different guises in organisations all around the world. It's easy to appreciate how unmotivated and frustrated leaders and talented people become from being held down by rules, procedures and overly controlling management. How often do you see management in organisations using systems and computers to build control, compliance and conformity into their businesses or projects, and then discover often too late that they have stifled the very creativity, intuition and imagination that is needed be successful?

Oracle Team won because, metaphorically speaking, the "tortoise", in the form of a controlling Oracle, released the "hare" – the sailors – to perform without further constraint and to engage fully in a quest they now found motivational, impossible and meaningful.

Control, compliance and conformity are often the very thing squashing and killing the imagination people need to be successful in a world full of disruption. This is why smaller, more entrepreneurial companies are often more successful when embarking on quests to disrupt industries. They are on quests to make a difference, to shake thing up and as immature companies they lack the systems and the resources and management expertise to control the outcome. Start-ups rely on being curious, creative and using imagination to open up new markets. Once they become larger and more successful, they lose the appetite for risk and seek sanctuary in systems of control that stifle, even kill the power of quest. But it does not have to be this way. Successful questers like Thiel, Thrun, Sergey Brin and Larry Page, Cummins and Büsser embraced the qualities and attributes of the quest and benefitted from building creative, passionate and imaginative organisations.

Discover your quest, define your target destination in clear, unambiguous outcomes-focused terms and then free your best talent to deliver meaningful benefits as they venture out on one questing adventure after the next.

Chapter Nine

Wrong Destination, Right Idea

"Unless we get fusion to work in some fashion, we are doomed, aren't we?"
Martin Fleischmann

1.

Situated on the banks of where the rivers Ohře and Teplá converge lies the beautiful spa town of Carlsbad, named after Charles IV, Holy Roman Emperor and Czech king. Carlsbad is famous for therapeutic hot springs and is visited by royalty and European aristocracy alike. The composer Ludwig van Beethoven was a frequent visitor who came for spa treatments and he would often take walks with the poet Goethe, much to the delight of the local people. Martin Fleischman, too, was born here on 29 March 1927. His life story was an adventure worthy of a Hollywood movie and he is best known for the scientific ignominy of the 20th century, the so-called star-in-a-bottle experiment.

In the late 1980s Fleischmann and colleague Stanley Pons announced to the world with much fanfare that they had achieved fusion at room temperature. Fusion, you will remember from Chapter Four, is the process that powers stars and was believed to require temperatures in excess of 100 million degrees centigrade and also massive machines. As such, the claim that this was being achieved at the other end of the spectrum, at room temperature in a laboratory, was big news and within days Fleischman and Pons were courting the world's media. Little did they imagine the storm that was about to break but perhaps Fleischmann's background prepared him for naysayers.

2.

Fleischmann often joked that by the age of 11, he'd had the dubious pleasure of being arrested by the Gestapo, not once but twice. Fleischmann's formative years coincided with a dark period in Carlsbad's history, a period that Fleischmann found difficult to talk about. "These things tend to concentrate your mind somewhat, you know, and my father was very badly beaten up by the Nazis. However, we got out."

His parents, Margaret Elizabeth Srb and Hans Fleischmann, met when Hans was stationed on duty at the Royal Castle in Tesin during World War One. Hans was a well-known officer in the Egerland Division, a guard's regiment and Margaret's father was an advisor to, and friend of, Emperor Franz Joseph of Austria. Hans Fleischmann's father, Maximillian had been adopted by a Jewish family – hence the name. The couple courted and were married as Roman Catholics. A daughter, Susi was born in 1923, and Martin followed four years later. Dr Hans Fleischmann distinguished himself as a lawyer and the family were well known and respected in Carlsbad, living comfortably and happily. Dark clouds were growing over Europe and in 1938, following the occupation of Czechoslovakia by Nazi Germany, the Nazis began to pursue the Fleischmann family. This was largely as a result of his family's Jewish name and because Hans was an anti-Nazi lawyer. Together with lifelong friend Dr Otto Fleischner, Hans was arrested, tortured and severely beaten by the Gestapo. When they were finished with him, Hans was taken to hospital with serious back injuries and his friend Dr Otto Fleischner was sent to Dachau Concentration Camp. As soon as Hans was well enough to travel, the Fleischmann family began their flight to freedom, taking no possessions. They were driven into the unoccupied part of Bohemia by Mr Grimm, an ex-fighter pilot from the Austrian air force, Hans's former old comrade-in-arms from the First World War. As a war hero, Hans still had friends who were prepared to put their lives on the line and get him and his family away to safety. "That was the first time we got away," recounts Martin Fleischmann. As the Nazi's expanded their occupation of

Czechoslovakia, the Fleischmann family were forced to consider their next route of escape. "It wasn't clear where. We might have gone to Canada or Argentina or South Wales, actually," says Martin. Fervent negotiations and planning found permanent English foster homes for Susi and Martin and the parents also received permission to come to England.

The next stage of the trip was the most dangerous, travelling by train across Germany to Holland. Just metres from the Dutch border and tantalisingly close to freedom the train was stopped and systematically searched, carriage by carriage. "We were in the last coach," says Martin, and my father Hans said, "No, sit tight, don't get off the train," and moments later, mercifully, the train pulled out of the station, just before the Nazi's reached them. "So that's how we got away the second time, and arrived at Liverpool Street Station in London, with 27 shillings and sixpence [about £1.37 in today's money] between the four of us."

3.

At the age of 12 and knowing very little English, Martin Fleischmann entered Worthing High School in the autumn of 1939. Sitting on the steps of his new home he said to himself "nobody owes you a living; there is only one way to go – namely up". Four years after escaping the Nazis, the local newspaper reported that Martin Fleischmann "had gained remarkable success in his Cambridge School Certificate examinations". He passed nine examination subjects and gained "A" passes in seven of them. For Fleischmann the doors to a better life opened and he completed his higher education at Imperial College, London. Fleischmann became a prominent electrochemist. He became president of the International Society of Electrochemists; was awarded the Royal Society of Chemistry's medal for electrochemistry and thermodynamics; and was elected as a fellow of the Royal Society, an honour given only to the most distinguished of scientists.

On 23 March 1989 Fleischmann, along with associate Stanley Pons, announced to the world's media that in an experiment conducted at room temperature in little more than a glass beaker, they had generated fusion. Nuclear fusion as opposed to nuclear fission – the process used to split the atom – was not new, scientist had been trying to harness its awesome power for decades. But up until this stage scientists had only generated hot fusion by smashing atoms together at outrageously high temperatures and pressure, until they fused together emitting vast amounts of energy. However, no method or machine had been devised to retain the immensely energetic process long enough to produce a net power outage. Astonishingly, Fleischmann and Pons claimed their process had done exactly this. Cold fusion was big news and the world's media rushed to hear more. Within a week of their announcement pictures of the scientists and the experiment festooned the front pages of *The Wall Street Journal*, *Time Magazine*, *Newsweek* and *Business Week*.

Any scientist who unlocked the door to solving the secrets of fusion and harnessed its tremendous power would gain prominence alongside Einstein and conceivably be revered for centuries to come. They would be awarded not only a Nobel Prize for Physics but a Peace Prize as well. Fame and fortune from licensing the process for commercial energy endeavours would follow. Fleishmann himself estimated trillions dollars would be made globally from this fusion technology. Tantalisingly, Fleischmann and Pond's cold-fusion discovery offered the potential to power the world's energy needs for the next million years. They imagined a day when every house would have a machine-made miniature "star-in-a-bottle" powering all energy requirements.

Then the critics descended. Within days of the announcement, universities around the world attempted to repeat Fleischmann's experiment, but with no success. For a moment there was a flurry of excitement when a university in Beijing claim to support Fleischmann's findings, but then they retracted the claim. The fall from grace was swift and brutal as critic upon critic joined the uproar. Part of the challenge for Pons and Fleischmann was the University of Utah, which wanted to protect its commercial rights and was limiting the amount of information the pair could release. By ignoring scientific protocol and going straight to the press before publishing the findings in scientific journals, the scientific community's response was cold and scornful. Unable to replicate the results of their experiment both Pons and Fleischmann were exiled to the scientific wilderness.

Fleischmann and Pons were never able to repeat the results they swore they had observed. The two partnered with Toyota and worked at a research lab in France trying vainly to replicate their experiment but their quest had come to an end. The debate around the legitimacy of what they observed in their cold-fusion experiment still rages today. In 1993 the nuclear scientist John R. Huizenga wrote the book *Cold Fusion: The Scientific Fiasco of the Century*. It was one of many attacks they had to endure.

Fleischmann was a fighter, a man whose life experiences had taught him the importance of self-belief and tenacity, but he also demonstrated a huge degree of grace and humility. "Many a time in my life I have been accused of coming up with crazy ideas." In the end he never cracked the code for cold fusion, but he was well respected for the role he played as an electrophysicist and in discovering the principle of surface-enhanced Raman spectroscopy, examining metal surfaces at a molecular level. Fleischmann passed away in 2012, and his manner to the end was calm, expressing regret at how things had worked out but showing no signs of anger. "Unless we get fusion to work in some fashion, we are doomed, aren't we?" he said in one of his last interviews.

Most of Fleischmann life had been a quest – the early years escaping from the grips of the Gestapo, fleeing to England as a refugee, working hard to become a respected electrophysicist; everything helped Fleischmann to recognise the importance of challenging the impossible. Fleischmann's endeavours also heightened an awareness of the importance of the quest to solve the world's energy requirements. Regardless of the validity of his claims Fleischmann was on a quest to find a solution for a limitless supply of pollution-free power that would meet the world's insatiable hunger for energy. It was a noble quest and it's important to note, not all quests end in success. Many fail, but each quest that fails takes humanity one step closer towards success. For this reason alone we owe thanks to this great adventurer for he showed us that even if you fail at your crazily impossible ideas it's better to fail trying than to never have tried at all.

Chapter Ten

Right Destination, Right Idea

"We were lucky enough to grow up in an environment where there was always much encouragement to children to pursue intellectual interests; to investigate what ever aroused curiosity."
Orville Wright

1.

It's hard even to consider a world without flight. In fact, jumping on a plane for a meeting across the country or across the world is so commonplace, that we forget how revolutionary a concept it would have been in the early 1900s. And so even when on 17 December 1903, the Wright brothers finally succeeded in making the first controlled, powered and sustained heavier-than-air human flight, it took some years for the world to take them seriously or even believe them at all. In fact they endured a great many years of being the butt of countless jokes at the time. This was one of the many challenges they faced, but as archetypal questers, Wilbur and Orville were sustained by their belief in the impossible, and by their faith that they would be the ones to beat the odds and deliver meaningful benefits to the world. Their destination: human flight.

Wilbur and Orville Wright were born in Dayton, Ohio into a family of five siblings who survived to adulthood. However, together with their sister Katharine, they were closer in age than their older brothers Lorin and Reuchlin and as David McCullough describes in his fascinating biography *The Wright Brothers*, the boys were inseparable. Not as loudly lauded perhaps, was Katharine, who joined their quest and dedicated much of her life to achieving it as well, playing a supportive role and nursing Orville after a terrible flying accident in 1908. This, incidentally earned his passenger Lieutenant Selfridge the dubious honour of being the first person to die in a crash of a powered airplane – proof again of the Wrights' own bravery in taking a quest on that did not just threaten their reputations, but also their lives.

Like many of the other questers you have met in this book, the Wrights faced failure time and time again. In fact, at times they grew so despondent about their cause that Wilbur, the older brother by four years admitted: "I confess that in 1901 I said to my brother Orville that man would not fly for fifty years." But they kept true to their destination having learnt the art of learning from failure extremely young. As little boys, their father the Reverend Milton Wright bought them a little toy from Paris. This "helicoptère", was based on an invention by French aeronautical pioneer Alphonse Pénaud and was made out of cork, bamboo and paper. A rubber band acted as its "engine" rotating its twin blades. Fascinated and impassioned by their first steps into aeronautics – they tried for many years to build their own upscaled versions but were never satisfied with the results. This did not defeat them, though, they moved onto kites and then gliders.

Wilbur first started discovering international questers for flight when reading to Orville who was struck down by typhoid. One of these questers, German aviator Otto Lilienthal died in a glider crash in 1896. A more cautious person might have been discouraged by this. Instead the Wright brothers were inspired to start their own experiments with flight, building on Lilienthal's knowledge and failures. Said Wilbur of Lilienthal in 1912: "No one equaled him in power to draw new recruits to the cause;... He presented the cause of human flight to his readers so earnestly, so attractively, and so convincingly that it was difficult for anyone to resist the temptation to make an attempt at it himself, ... he was without question the greatest of the precursors, and the world owes to him a great debt."

2.

Both the Wright brothers were self-taught engineers. An extensive library and family love of reading were their greatest assets. Says

McCullough "Wilbur and Orville grew up in a house where there was no indoor plumbing, no electricity, and no telephone. But there were a lot of books." For a living, they repaired bicycles and later sold photographic equipment, but their passion was what humans had long dreamt of mastering: flight. Said Orville of that time, "The public, discouraged by the failures and tragedies just witnessed, considered flight beyond the reach of man, and classed its adherents with the inventors of perpetual motion. We began our active experiments at the close of this period…"

Determined to develop their own successful design, Wilbur and Orville headed to Kitty Hawk, North Carolina, where heavy winds were more conducive to flying. It would be here that they would fail many, many times, but at the same time bring supporters into their ambit – despite their failures. The most important of these – and there were many – would be: Octave Chanute an American civil engineer and aviation pioneer, who would advise and mentor them, but who they would eventually surpass; their family especially the Reverend, who supported them with a hefty $1000 corpus fund and the third party of their "trio", Katharine; and William Tate, the postmaster at Kitty Hawk who would open his home to them and assist them in many ways in their early experiments. Finally, there was unsung hero Charlie Taylor, who managed their bicycle shop, helping to ensure their continued income. He also successfully built the aluminium engine for the Wrights' plane when no car company could supply one.

Said Wilbur, "What one man can do himself directly is but little. If, however, he can stir up ten others to take up the task he has accomplished much." Imagining human flight was a powerful fictional story, and through the power of imagination, which as illustrated in Chapter Eight, Harari believes sets humans apart from other species, the Wright Brothers were able to inspire people to join and support them on their quest for human flight. It was French explorer, writer, poet, and pioneering aviator Antoine de Saint-Exupéry who said, "if you want to build a flotilla of ships, you don't sit around talking about carpentry. No, you need to set people's souls ablaze with visions of exploring distant shores." This definitely proved to be the case for Orville and Wilbur and is one of the powers of being on a quest. People are naturally inspired to join and contribute to it.

3.

Through his own research, Wilbur established that there were three elements required to build a successful flying machine: wings for lift, a method of control for the pilot and a power source or propulsion. And because of their extensive experience with the bicycle, which they knew to be highly unstable but controllable, the Wrights saw no reason why an airplane could not be unstable yet controllable as well. But they needed to be in control of three actions of motion: pitch, roll and yaw. Wilbur and Orville initially built gliders to fly at Kitty Hawk. Said Wilbur, "In studying their failures we found many points of interest to us."

And fail they did. Their first field experiments began in September to October of 1900. These continued over the next three years: 1901 (July–August); 1902 (September–October); and 1903 (October–December). Their first manned glider flight was disappointing to say the least. Based on Lilienthal's calculations, the glider did not achieve the lift their aviation pioneer had predicted. Though they had broken the record for distance in gliding and their results were better than had been achieved before, Wilbur wrote: "when we looked at the time and money which we had expended, and considered the progress made and the distance yet to go, we considered our experiments a failure. At this time I made the prediction that men would sometime fly, but that it would not be within our lifetime."

The power of a clearly defined target destination is a crucial requirement on any journey, especially journeys into the unknown that will involve failures and setbacks. Recalculating a new route is part of the process on quests. When embarking on journeys other people consider impossible, one will inevitably end up being blocked by a few dead-ends. The destination serves to help teams refocus and renew their commitment. There will always be the naysayers, those who do not believe or want the quest to succeed, because success ushers in new powerful paradigms. But questers are able to use their destination to keep them tracking forward in the general right direction until they achieve breakthrough.

Such is the case with the Wright brothers. Despite Wilbur's gloomy prediction, they continued to work on their quest, the quest that Wilbur would describe to Chanute as his "disease". They were patient but they were also thorough. Their strategy? Trial and error – experimentation. This included even the construction of their own wind tunnels to test wings of different shapes for the pressures and forces acting on them. They used the data they collected from these experiments to see where earlier calculations had been incorrect. Another important step in realising their goal was their study of buzzards and other birds in flight. Wilbur and Orville watched how birds angled their wings for balance and control, and emulating this developed what they called "wing warping" – an innovative new design for wings. The Wrights also added a moveable rudder. Arguably their greatest innovation was three-axis control to bank, turn and elevate or descend. These combinations enabled the pilot to steer the aircraft effectively and to maintain its balance – a principle still used in aeroplanes today.

Says McCullough, "Wilbur Wright was a genius. Orville was exceptional in his inventive talents as well. They were also incredibly courageous. We have to remember that every time they went up on one of their experimental flights they were risking their lives. They were so aware of this that the brothers refused to go up together so that if one was killed, the other could still carry on their mission. They were so driven by their belief, confidence, and determination to succeed. They took on this mission the way some people would follow a religious conviction. They had a cause and they would not give up; they never let failure or disappointment discourage them. If knocked down, they got back up on their feet and kept going. Call it perseverance, call it determination, call it gumption, call it what you will."

On the day they finally flew their glider at Kitty Hawk a record 620 feet, they were able to record notes and use photography to improve on their design. The Wrights also built a new wind tunnel to do more experiments when they returned home to Dayton. They used all this new data to build a propeller and an engine for their first flying machine, which they called a "Flyer".

Though Wilbur won the coin toss to test the Flyer first, the engine stalled on take-off. True to form, the Wrights simply repaired their flying machine and Orville took off on December 17, 1903. The flight lasted only 12 seconds and was largely unremarked upon, but it was the beginning of something incredible – some had even said impossible. Of four flights they made that day, the longest was 59 seconds, over a distance of 852 feet against a 20-mile wind. Said McCullough, "They knew then, they had the secret to it, the technique. It wasn't just that they had invented a machine; they knew how to fly it."

Despite this, their Flyer was underpowered and difficult to control. The brothers knew they still had a lot to do before their invention would be perfect. As such, they set up the world's first test-flight facilities at Huffman Prairie, flying time after time for two years. By doing this, they were able to fine-tune and experiment, dealing with various challenging malfunctions until they could produce a plane capable of flying for extended periods of time and operating under the complete control of a trained pilot. Though they started by only achieving a minute in a straight line, by 1905 they could fly for more than half an hour, or until they ran out of fuel. At this point, they realised they had produced a viable flying machine.

4.

Though the Wright brothers should have found immediate acclaim in their own country – it took crossing to Europe in 1908 to achieve this. In the US, many still believed them to be crackpots. The US government had also recently funded numerous failed flying experiments, and unlike the Wrights, were reluctant to ignore these failures. In France, Wilbur made many public flights and gave rides to officials, journalists, potential investors, kings and statesmen while in Washington D.C. Orville did his own flying demonstrations – one of which included the calamitous flight where the propeller fell off and Lieutenant Selfridge lost his life. This was a tragedy that ironically only stopped Orville temporarily while he recovered with Katharine at his bedside. Wilbur continued his flights in Le Mans, France, although thoroughly shocked by the tragedy.

In time, they managed to secure contracts for aeroplanes in Europe and eventually achieved recognition in the US, receiving medals from the US President William Taft and the French government. They were international sensations; and when they got back to Dayton, this was acknowledged by a parade in their honour. American industrialist J.P. Morgan, also assisted the brothers in establishing the Wright Company – their own aircraft-manufacturing company in 1910.

Unfortunately, this was not the last of their battles. The moment their knowledge become more public, the Wrights would have to defend their first US patent, 821,393 (in 1906), which claimed their invention of a system of aerodynamic control that manipulated a flying machine's surfaces. Until Wilbur's death, he would fight patent infringement after patent infringement. It was time consuming, uncreative and exhausting, but they won every single case in American courts – proof once again that they had never deviated from their own True North.

5.

Said Darrel Collins, US Park Service, Kitty Hawk National Historical Park, "Before the Wright Brothers, no one in aviation did anything fundamentally right. Since the Wright Brothers, no one has done anything fundamentally different." Much of what we consider to be aeronautics today has been built on their inspiration, risk and experiments. They solved the problem of flight and left future generations to refine their designs. But Orville, who would live to see his invention used in war and wreak havoc with it, was disturbed that the "meaningful difference" he and Wilbur had sought had taken on a new, darker side. But this had already been foreshadowed by Major General Baden Powell, the then President of the Aeronautical Society of Britain who'd said of their ability to fly, "That Wilbur Wright is in possession of a power which controls the fate of nations is beyond dispute."

The ripple effects of flight cannot be overestimated. Said McCullough, "Very few people have so dramatically changed the world by what they achieved, as did the Wright brothers. Consider that they flew for the first time in 1903 and that last year alone 70 million people flew in and out of the O'Hare airport in Chicago. The role of the airplane is ubiquitous, and we take it all for granted that it was not so long ago in the grand scheme of time that this amazing thing was invented."

6.

On May 25, 1910 Orville's 82-year-old father would join him for the single flight of his life. On the same day, Orville flew for six minutes with his big brother as his passenger – marking the first and only flight the siblings would make together. One can only imagine the joy of that flight and the knowledge that, despite their many failures, they had finally reached their quest's final destination.

They were flying.

Final Thoughts

How big is the hole you will leave behind?

"Twenty years from now you will be more disappointed by the things that you didn't do than by the ones you did do. So throw off the bowlines. Sail away from the safe harbour. Catch the trade winds in your sails. Explore. Dream. Discover."
Mark Twain

1.

The poet and philosopher Henry David Thoreau said, "Most men live lives of quiet desperation and go to the grave with the song still in them." *Quest* is a book about questers – people and organisations that choose to sing their song and make a meaningful difference by challenging the boundaries of impossibility. It has shared the stories of the amazing and even magical things that happen when people and organisations embark on audacious adventures to build a better future. As I have shown in *Quest,* you do not have to be on a grand stage to benefit from the powerful leadership force of a quest. The framework developed around the three qualities of a quest is equally applicable to even personal quests. For example, writing this book became a personal quest, one that, although I did not realise it at the time, was shaped and inspired by the events of a fateful Easter weekend in 1993, in South Africa, the country of my birth. Here is the story of what happened and how it shaped *Quest*.

2.

The day that changed everything began like most Saturday mornings. In many ways it was the perfect African morning, a refreshing coolness in the air holding back the heat of the day as the sun rose higher. It had seemed sure to be another beautiful day in Africa when the leader of the South African Communist Party, Chris Hani, headed out to buy the morning paper at a nearby shopping mall. His wife Limpho, and daughters Neo and Lindiwe were away visiting relatives over the Easter weekend and he'd briefly left at home his 15-year-old daughter Nomakhwezi. At the time South Africa was in the middle of its precarious political transition. Hani had been working long hours over the previous weeks negotiating the country's new constitution and he'd been looking forward to a quiet weekend spending time with Nomakhwezi. That day he was going to be all hers; he'd promised.

When Polish immigrant and karate devotee Janusz Waluz found his dojo empty, he realised with annoyance that it was closed for Easter Saturday. So Waluz used his spare time to head off to the local Gun Exchange and emerged with 25 rounds of 9 mm subsonic ammunition. He now had one more task before returning home, to stake out the house of Chris Hani – number three on a hit list that had been drawn up by a group of white supremacists and given to Waluz, their hitman.

Driving his red Ford Laser, he came up to the gentle bend in the road where Hani lived and as he slowly approached he noticed Hani pulling out of the driveway and driving away. Waluz floored the pedal to catch up; he prided himself on being a rally driver and used his skills to quickly manoeuvre behind Hani's car. Hani entered a shopping mall and parked, unaware he had been followed. Waluz double-checked and noticed Hani's bodyguards were not present. This left him with a dilemma; he'd not planned to carry out the killing that day nor did he want to shoot Hani in a highly visible and populated shopping mall. He made a snap decision and raced back to Hani's house, coaxing himself to seize the opportunity in front of him. An opportunity like this would not come around again; he stopped his car outside the house, pulled on his gloves and waited.

As soon as Hani returned home, Waluz approached him. "I didn't want to shoot him in the back," Waluz recounted later of his evil deed. "So I called, 'Mr Hani'. When he turned, I drew my pistol and shot him." Waluz stared down at the lifeless body calmly turned and walked away.

Across the road, Retha Harmse, Hani's neighbour witnessed the shooting. Before she could do anything, it was all over. With an arrogant stride, Waluz climbed back into his car and drove off. As quickly as possible, Retha ran into her house and picked up the phone to call the police; she had memorised the car's number plates. Police on patrol were quickly radioed and within minutes they had Waluz's car boxed in. His blood-splattered clothes and smoking gun were evidence of what he'd done.

For Mandela, South Africa's great leader, this assassination was a huge blow. He recalls in his book *A Long Walk to Freedom,* that at the time of Hani's death, "the country was fragile". That night Nelson Mandela went on TV to address the nation, calling for calm and restraint. He pointed out that it was the quick action of an Afrikaner woman, the very ethnic group that Waluz believed he epitomised, which had led to the killer being apprehended. Mandela's speech touched the hearts of mourners and fearful South Africans alike as he said:

"Today, an unforgivable crime has been committed... a crime against a dearly beloved son of our soil... We are a nation deeply wounded... we must not permit ourselves to be provoked by those who seek to deny us the very freedom Chris Hani gave his life for. Let us respond with dignity and in a disciplined fashion... The ANC dips its banner in salute to this outstanding son of Africa."

Almost three decades earlier in 1964, Mandela had given a speech now known as *I Am Prepared To Die.* This three-hour-long oration was given from the dock of the defendant at the Rivonia Trial, arguably the most significant political trial in South Africa's history. During the speech made to a watchful world Mandela eloquently and masterfully announced his own personal quest: "During my lifetime I have dedicated my life to this struggle of the African people. I have fought against white domination, and I have fought against black domination. I have cherished the ideal of a democratic and free society in which all persons will live together in harmony and with equal opportunities. It is an ideal for which I hope to live for and to see realised. But, My Lord, if it needs be, it is an ideal for which I am prepared to die." At the end of the trial Mandela was convicted of sabotage against the State and sentenced to life imprisonment. He would serve 27 years of the sentence before being freed in February 1990.

It was not Mandela's desire to become a martyr, dying for his cause. Mandela's quest was "for a democratic and free society" and by announcing this quest to the world, he, metaphorically speaking, created a destination for himself and fellow questers to journey towards as they battled against the tyranny of apartheid. Had Mandela's goal been to win power and leadership of the country, the outcome and miracle of South Africa's transition from apartheid to democracy would've been starkly different. But Mandela was on a noble quest that would benefit millions and his quest became a guiding beacon and the True North from which he never deviated.

Never before, though, had his quest been more tested than at the time of Hani's assassination; these were some of the country's darkest days. Mandela said he was, "concerned that Hani's death might trigger a racial war, with the youth deciding that their hero should become a martyr for whom they would lay down their own lives". The pressure was mounting on Mandela to withdraw from negotiations with South Africa's white ruling party and to heed the call for an armed revolution. The white government had little international support and there were those around Mandela who were calling for a military victory. But a civil war would not result in a democratic and free society and Mandela knew this.

To stay true to his quest, in his autobiography Mandela tells how he instigated two important strategies. Firstly, "in order to forestall outbreaks of retaliatory violence, he arranged a week-long series of mass rallies and demonstrations throughout the country. This would give people a means of expressing their frustration without resorting to violence". Secondly, he collaborated with his political enemy, the leader of the ruling white party: "Mr de Klerk and I spoke privately and agreed that we would not let Hani's murder derail the negotiations," said Mandela.

The assassination of Chris Hani sent South Africa into a state of shock as people from all races looked into a dark abyss. The fragile peace talks hung by a thread. In the days leading up to Hani's funeral, tensions threatened to explode. He was a living legend, a courageous freedom fighter, military commander and a fiery, passionate orator who could bring crowds cheering to their feet. A confidential cable written by a US diplomat just before the assassination and leaked to the public through Julian Assange's Wikileaks in 2013, stated: "Hani appears on public platforms in the townships wearing quasi-combat fatigues and delivering fiery speeches that arouse and delight the audience." In Hani, the killers had chosen the perfect victim to raise an inferno of fury.

A deeply saddened Archbishop Desmond Tutu said, "I fear for our country. Chris Hani, more than anyone else, had the credibility among the young to rein in the radicals." Tutu understood the pulse of the country. If he feared a civil explosion there seemed little hope. Hani was immensely popular especially amongst the "young lions" – comrades who were on the front line of apartheid's battleground.

At the time of Hani's death I was a university graduate working in the strategy and innovations unit of a leading financial services group. The death of Chris Hani had a huge impact on me; I was saddened, shocked and angered. If it came to civil war I would be compelled to fight with the ANC for the dream of a democratic and free South Africa. Not all South African whites feared or resisted the end of apartheid. I looked out of my office window; there had been news of mass demonstrations across the country and as midday approached so did the tens of thousands of black warriors swarming through the streets of Johannesburg. Their cries "*Amandla Awethu*" – Power to the People – echoed through the streets and the throb of helicopters hovering above the crowds made the air thick with tension. Looking out the window from the sanctuary of my office I could see the procession surging through the streets below. Compelled by Mandela's words I joined a procession of fellow South Africans. I was swept up in a sea of monumental emotions, carried away by a chanting, heaving, mourning crowd. It was one of the most frightening, exhilarating and uplifting experiences of my life.

The horrors of that Easter weekend in 1993 had a profound and unexpected impact on South Africa's future. Rather than throw the country into a bitter and crippling civil war, as the killers had hoped it would, within a year of Hani's death South Africans, regardless of colour, race or creed voted in the country's first democratic elections.

How did South Africa escape the ravages of a civil war that so many countries in similar situations have been unable to avoid? If you compare and contrast the unrest and civil wars in Rwanda, Ukraine, Syria, Libya, Afghanistan and Iraq's conflict with Islamic States, then what South Africa achieved was nothing short of a miracle. Something was at work that made the impossible, possible. The peaceful change in South Africa was no doubt due to the extraordinary leadership and vision of Nelson Mandela. Much has been written about his exemplary leadership skills. But, there was also a powerful disruptive force at play that was even bigger than the great man himself.

Following extensive studies of organisations that have embarked on truly world-changing journeys and reflecting on the events that transpired over that ill-fated Easter weekend in 1993, I have come to a realisation. South Africa and the organisations I studied have benefitted from the power and the inspiration of a leader's quest. In Mandela's case his quest evidences all three qualities of a quest. The first quality is the power of delivering meaningful benefits – achieving his quest resulted in a significant and meaningful difference to the lives of millions of disenfranchised South Africans. The second quality is the power of achieving the impossible – many believed Mandela's quest to be an idealistic endeavour, crazy and unachievable. But as Mandela said, "It always seems impossible until it's done." The third quality is the power of a target destination. Mandela's destination was exceptionally clear – a democratic South Africa, free of black or white domination. His destination was devoid of ambiguity and it influenced all his actions and decisions, even after he became president of South Africa. Leaders that follow on from Mandela could do well to understand the power of quest.

3.

Imagine if you, your team, your organisation or your community embraced a culture of questing. Now imagine if we could create a questing culture everywhere. What if through the power of knowing the target destination, inspired by the possibility of achieving the impossible and delivering meaningful benefits, we could empower people everywhere to have the courage and conviction to do their small bit or big bit to change the world? What if through the power of quest we created a culture where people believed they could make a difference? We would craft more wholesome and inspiring jobs, truly ethical businesses, value-enhancing business models, healthier economies and more opportunities to contribute well-being in the world.

When on September 2015 Michael Horn, the American boss of Volkswagen said: "We have totally screwed up," he was apologising for the cheat device that Volkswagen engineers had used to trick emission tests. The largest transgression to rock the corporate world since the bank sector's inter-bank interest-rate-fixing Libor scandal and BP's Deepwater Horizon oil spill. Engineers at Volkswagen decided to create emissions-cheating devices by programming an algorithm, a few lines of smart code, into the cars' software. The cheat device would detect when the car was being tested under laboratory conditions and commanded the diesel cars' electronic brains to circumvent emissions testing.

In 2007, the now ousted CEO of the Volkswagen Group, Martin Winterkorn, proclaimed his sales goal was to surpass 10 million units per year by 2018. Commentators argued that the strategy was too bold and ambitious for a company that was at that point only selling about six million units a year. Winterkorn was resolute; he wanted Volkswagen to become the largest automobile company during his tenure. In 2014, Winterkorn proudly announced to shareholders his strategy to be a success. He achieved his goal, four years ahead of the planned schedule. Volkswagen had become the world's largest car company and the first motor manufacturer to reach 10 million unit sales in a year. Winterkorn was the toast of the stock market, except we know now the real cost of his strategy – not only to the Volkswagen brand and shareholders but also to society. During the first five years of Winterkorn's strategy, the Volkswagen Group drove business units relentlessly to focus on sales. This strategy resulted in an increase in sales of nearly 50 percent compared with 2007. It is plausible to assume that the pressure placed on regional and sales heads to hit stretch targets was considerable and this pressure resulted in absolutely unbeneficial behaviour. By 2015 the rot caused by Winterkorn's ambitious growth strategy began to surface in the ugly guise of the cheat-device scandal.

Olaf Lies, a Volkswagen board member, told the BBC in an interview, "We only found out about the problems in the last board meeting, shortly before the media did... Those people who allowed this to happen, or who made the decision to install this software – they acted criminally. They must take personal responsibility."

Mr Lies' statement is understandable but here in blinding daylight is the problem with how organisations are being managed and executives are motivated and rewarded.

The knee-jerk reaction is for more control, greater compliance and further conformity. What Mr Lies seeks is the equivalent of a corporate Band-Aid. If Volkswagen only seeks out individuals or groups for punishment all that happens is they address the symptoms and not the causes of the disease.

Responsibility goes all the way to the top and sits with the Volkswagen Board who agreed the corporate strategy. Their strategy shaped

Volkswagen's corporate culture and ultimately the pitiable behaviour and belief that cheating the Environmental Protection Agency to improve car unit sales was not only acceptable but also the preferred approach to hitting sales targets. The Volkswagen scandal is the result of a systematic failure of modern-day capitalism and a management mindset that seeks to protect the prevailing paradigm of shareholder maximisation at the expense of the broader society.

Recent corporate scandals are representative of a long depressing list. If leaders only focus on short-term shareholder value, quarterly sales and the bottom line, in a continuous battle to be the biggest, then the people they employ will focus on just the figures and not the awesome value creation that is possible when organisations embark on quests to deliver meaningful benefits. If Volkswagen's executives had been on a quest to deliver greater and more meaningful benefits to motorists – in the form of say lower actual emissions – this scandal would not have erupted. But Volkswagen's executives did not adopt a strategy that included a quest to deliver meaningful benefits and create shared value. Volkswagen sought to be the biggest and that in itself is not a quest nor does it deliver meaningful benefits to the world. There sits Volkswagen's downfall, Mr Lies.

Like Volkswagen, Google also achieved the status of being the world's biggest, albeit as an online search company. But this achievement is a result of implementing strategies that delivering meaningful benefits, rather than following a strategy to just be the biggest. Google dominates because its leaders and corporate culture is all about embarking on quests, those bold crazy strategies that make a difference. On 10th August 2015, Larry Page, the co-founder of Google, announced in a letter to Googlers and investors the launch of Alphabet, Google's new holding company. "From the start, we've always strived to do more," said Page, "and to do important and meaningful things with the resources we have. We did a lot of things that seemed crazy at the time. Many of those crazy things now have over a billion users, like Google Maps, YouTube, Chrome, and Android. And we haven't stopped there. We are still trying to do things other people think are crazy but we are super excited about." From quests like Google self-driving cars, to Google's Life Sciences – a quest to develop a glucose-sensing contact lens – and Calico, Google's longevity company working on the quest to crack the ageing code – perhaps this is the ultimate of all quests, if we end aging that would be an incredible feat – Google implements questing strategies that deliver meaningful benefits. In his letter, Page conveys the essence of what it means to be a questing organisation – a deep, heartfelt, emotional commitment to achieving an outcome for oneself and the greater good. The move to launch Alphabet is a brilliant strategy that allows the company to increasingly focus on quests that deliver meaningful benefits. Google is not immune to controversy, but on the whole the quests that Google embarks on promise to take society to higher levels.

4.

How big is the hole you or your organisation will leave behind? Not for your family or the people employed by your organisation, naturally the hole would be huge for them. Rather how big would the hole be for the world or community you touch and influence? When Mandela stepped away from running South Africa he left a gaping hole that has not been filled by the politicians and leaders who have followed. If Third Rock Ventures, Peter Thiel, Elizabeth Holmes, Ocean Pleasant, Cathy Tie, Paul Cummins, Eléonor Picciotto, Virginie Meylan, Maximilian Büsser, Mark Zuckerberg, Larry Page, Sergey Brin, Brian Chesky, Elon Musk or any of the other questers and questing organisations profiled in this book disappeared, they too would leave behind huge holes.

This is because they each strive to deliver meaningful benefits to the communities they touch. So ask yourself the question: If your organisation was swallowed up, taken over by a competitor would people go: "They left a gaping hole", or would they say, "Nah, what hole?" In the UK where I now live, the companies that have recently disappeared include Woolworths, Jessops, Blockbuster and Kodak and were easy to forget because they peddled *products* not meaningful benefits to the world they served. Companies on quests create holes that competitors are unable to fill. It's an amazingly powerful strategy because it attracts the best talent and stumps competitors.

We are increasingly living in a world where questers are achieving extraordinary results. Questers are leaders who are driven to make a difference in the world. Do not confuse questers for philanthropists or goody two-shoes charity workers. Questers are hard-nosed capitalists who are results driven and obsessively focused on the bottom line. It's just their focus is not only on making profit; questers want to deliver meaningful benefits first and foremost. Making money is secondary and the outcome of a job well done. Take a closer look at the corporate superstars of today: Google, Facebook, Tesla motors and the organisations I have profiled in *Quest* and you will notice that the common attribute is a desire to achieve the impossible in a way that delivers meaningful benefits to the world. It is therefore not surprising that these companies, which are using what I term "questing strategies", are leading and defining the rules for success in a changing world.

Being a quester means you still need to be efficient, but not at the expense of delivering meaningful benefits for short-term gains. The world is lurching from one industry crisis or corporate scandal to another because of a short-termism myopia. Each scandal erodes shareholder and societal value. There are too many examples of a system that has gone wrong. Trillions of dollars spent bailing out banks during the Great Recession. Tesco a leading retail grocer in the UK; rocked by the horsemeat scandal and internal accounting transgressions and which is now struggling to regain its former glory. And, of course the motor industry, shuddering from the recent Volkswagen Dieselgate scandal.

It's not surprising that the citizens of the world have lost faith in leaders and corporations. But this presents an opportunity. Trust has now become a competitive advantage. Being on a quest that delivers meaningful benefits to the world, even just your world of influence, is a powerful way to build trust amongst stakeholders and gain advantage over competitors.

Implementing questing strategies is not easy. Quests involve pushing against established paradigms and entrenched dogmas. But as you will have seen in *Quest,* these strategies result in incredible returns – not just for the questers involved but for society and shareholders as well.

Larry Page uses the term "moonshots" to describe his questing innovations. At Google, Page encourages experimentation and the free flow of ideas for "all Googlers who share a desire to challenge what's possible". Most companies are "happy with 10 percent improvements," says Page who believes this essentially entails standing still and doing the same as everyone else. Page seeks improvements by a factor of 10. Thousand-percent improvement requires tackling problems with energy, vigour and commitment. It requires radically rethinking problems, exploring the edges and pushing the envelope of what is thought possible. It requires making the impossible possible with a resolute conviction that what you are doing will make a meaningful difference. These requirements are the quintessence of a leader's quest and this is why quests are such powerful change catalysts.

I'm buoyed by the fact that there is a vanguard of superstar questers who have already embarked on quests to find solutions that will reignite economic growth, create new jobs and solve many of the world's most pressing problems. But more questers are urgently needed to take advantages of the Age of Quests that is unfolding. While the majority of business leaders and entrepreneurs run around saying, "I'm going to improve the efficiencies on this or that existing product" or "I'm building a better social media app", questers go about identifying inefficiencies in systems that matter most to people. By looking for areas that are malfunctioning, they embark on quests that make a world of difference.

The challenges of the 21st century are too massive to be overcome by being creatively conservative and leading with an industrial manager's mindset of control, compliance and conformity. The manager's 3Cs need to be relinquished. Audacious rethinking and new solutions are required if this century is to be our greatest ever. Solutions will not come from the conservative centre occupied by an industrialised mindset. Individuals and organisations need to be set free and the power of the leadership quest, which has advanced society in the past, can be used to magnificent effect.

The power of quests can be found in how each quest binds teams, and informs and inspires people to work together to make bold positive differences. Quests attract the best talent; they empower people and unleash passion and energy. Quests give people a sense of purpose, which encourages creativity, experimentation and innovation. Quests deliver strategy at speed, by being agile and adaptable because when you know your target destination it's easy to reroute. Quests deliver sustainable competitive advantage.

We need to encourage more questers in our organisations, and to do this we need to "release the hare" from the controlling constraints of modern-day management. Quests are not about relinquishing control, however. Many of the greatest questers are self-confessed control freaks, but they understand how the power of a quest inspires people's imagination and channels their energy and engagement. When on a quest the most successful leaders appear to set wildly ambitious goals, they celebrate failure as an opportunity to unlearn and relearn new paradigms as quickly as they can, and they give their team members the autonomy required to rethink and innovate.

Our research at TomorrowToday Global shows that great strides forward are achieved when people and organisations embark on quests. By harnessing the qualities of a quest, leaders are able to unleash a powerful force of positive change. I have argued throughout *Quest* that humankind is where it is today because of the power of a quest. And, that is essentially the crux of this book – the power of a leader's quest.

I wanted to use the three qualities of a quest: delivering meaningful benefits, achieving the impossible and having a target destination, as a framework to share why quests have proven to be such powerful agents of change since the dawning of civilisation. And I hope to have demonstrated how leaders can leverage these qualities to embark on quests that mobilise their teams, organisations and customers as they journey towards success.

What's holding us back? The technology and capital know-how is all already there. Like the hare and the tortoise in Bennett's cartoon, described in *Quest's* prologue, what is being held prostrate is leadership. We are too fearful, too worried about taking risks; we spend too much time focusing on control, compliance and conformity. We do too much "me too" and don't attempt enough "moonshots". There is too much paranoia about the next quarter and the share price and not enough about delivering future longer-term benefits. But this is changing. There is a growing leadership and organisational trend of delivering benefits and attempting to achieve the impossible. *Quest* offers a framework for future success and the leaders catching this wave will be the winners of the 21st Century.

In 1989, while attending university to study law and economics, I remember watching the film *Dead Poets Society.* The late Robin Williams plays the role of John Keating, an English schoolteacher who uses unorthodox methods to reach out to his students. In one scene Mr Keating jumps up onto his classroom table and asks the question: "Why do I stand up here?" A student at the back of the classroom shouts out. "To feel taller." Mr Keating smiles, ringing a bell on his desk using his foot and responds by saying, "No! Thank you for playing, Mr. Dalton. I stand upon my desk to remind myself that we must constantly look at things in a different way. You see, the world looks very different from up here... Just when you think you know something, you have to look at it in another way. Even though it may seem silly or wrong, you must try! ... Dare to strike out and find new ground." What Mr Keating was teaching his students in that scene can be summed up in a quote by futurist and writer Alvin Toffler: "The illiterate of the twenty-first 21st century will not be those who cannot read and write, but those who cannot learn, unlearn, and relearn." Successful leaders in the 21st century look at things differently as they embark on quests that strike out and discover new ground from where they can build disruptive advantage.

Here is my personal quest: to build a better working world. It is a bold quest and one I'm dedicating myself to because if I can reach out to the audiences I speak to and influence only one business leader to embark on quests that address the real challenges of the 21st century, then it will have been a journey worth travelling. I hope to encourage and discover new ways of thinking, and to work with future-focused organisations and leaders exploring how they can commercially deliver meaningful benefits to the portions of the world they touch and influence. I passionately believe if more people try to improve the world and the communities they touch, then, like the example given in this book of GE's quest to improve the world by one percent every year, bit by bit it will all add up and the world will become a better place.

Dare to strike out, dare to find new ground and make your world this better place. Dare to embark on a quest for yourself, your team, your business and your world. As Sebastian Thrun says, "We should have more moonshots and flights to the moon in areas of societal importance." So set your sails, navigate away from your safe harbour. Explore. Dream. Discover. Be successful.

Acknowledgements

I AM GRATEFUL for the love, encouragement and support of my wife, Hayley during the long hours and early mornings writing this book, for her advice while reading and listening to continuous drafts of every chapter, and for her input in structuring and cracking the design and flow of the book. Love and thanks to my little boy Leo for his joyous smiles, incessant interruptions to watch "tractors" on my laptop while I was writing and reminding me to always stop to smell the roses. Special thanks to my family, who have afforded me the encouragement, love and conviction to embark on my own quest.

This book would not have been possible without the reinforcement and backing of my business partner Graeme Codrington who ten years ago boldly joined me to embark on a quest to take TomorrowToday to a truly global level with the opening of our UK & European office. Special thanks must also go out to Jackie Ronson who joined Graeme and me in the early days and readied our start-up for success. Special mention to my UK colleagues, both past and present, in particular Wendy Mauchline. It has been an exciting adventure that involved launching the business two years prior to the financial crises and successfully riding the wave of disruption that followed the greatest recession since the 1930s. It would never have been achieved without the passion and commitment of these extraordinary people.

My clients are an exceptional inspiration to my work. Deep gratitude goes out to Jo Kelly at the John Lewis Partnership for introducing me to the Partnership many years ago. The Partnership is my most admired client and it is the partners whose dedication, diligence and exceptional leadership skills always inspire me. I've thoroughly enjoyed working with all the partners who have attended my future-focused leadership boot camps and with whom I have shared many thought-provoking discussions. Special mentions to Ange Brook at Novartis, who has shared, partnered and contributed at times along my journey for which I am indeed thankful. I'm also indebted to the executive leadership programme directors at various business schools where I lecture. In particular the London Business School, including Liz-Anne Gayle and Lorraine Vaun-Davis; Dil Sidhu at the Manchester Business School; and Helen Chauveau and Thomas Hinterseer at the European Centre for Executive Development located on the INSEAD campus.

In particular very special gratitude goes out to the time afforded to me during my research into the quest for fusion energy – by all accounts the greatest scientific quest of the 21st century. The numerous experts who generously spent time in lengthy conversations, include: Steven Cowley, CEO of the UK atomic energy authority at the Culham Centre for Fusion Energy; and at ITER, the International Thermonuclear Experimental Reactor Organization – Rem Haange, Chief Operations Officer; Mr David Campbell, Head of Science and Operations; Akko Maas, Senior Engineering Officer; Sabina Griffith, Communications Officer and Ruxandra Pilsiu my tour guide around the amazing building site of Tokomak facility.

The formulation of thoughts, ideas and writing has benefited greatly from the wisdom and generosity of many others: my colleagues at TomorrowToday Global in particular Jude Foulston who works tirelessly with great infectious enthusiasm; my speaker agents, including Tim Gold, Nick Gold, Rebecca Matthews and Debbie Price at Speakers' Corner and Cosimo Turroturro at Speakers Associates.

And last but not least to my book editor Paula Marais who is an accomplished writer in her own right and whose guidance and assistance was unsurpassed. Special thanks goes to her for her assistance with researching and co-writing of the Poppies and Wright brothers chapters in *Quest.*

Thank you all!

Sources

Introduction And Chapter One

Bennett, Charles; The Fables Of Aesop; Bradbury & Evans; 1857

Dunsany, Lord; The True History Of The Tortoise And The Hare; Flash Fiction; 2008

Google's Original X-Man A Conversation With Sebastian Thrun; Foreign Affairs; November 2013

Lupkin, Sydney; People With 'Butterfly' Skin Condition Triumph Through Pain; ABC News; February 2013 Http://Abcnews.Go.Com/

The 100 Greatest Adventure Books Of All Time; National Geographic; Http://Www.Nationalgeographic.Com

Nanos, Janelle; The Cure: Third Rock Ventures' Ground-breaking Idea; Boston Magazine http://Www.Bostonmagazine.Com

Third Rock Ventures May Have The Cure To Get Ground-breaking Therapies To Patients Biospace: Life Sciences News Http://Www.Biospace.Com/

Chapter Two

Gertner, Jon Fast Company, Behind GE's Vision For The Industrial Internet Of Things Http://Www.Fastcompany.Com

Lewis, John, Spedan; Fairer Shares, A Possible Advance In Civilisation, Staples Press, 1954

Luttrell, David; Atkinson, Tyler And Rosenblum, Harvey; Federal Reserve Bank Of Dallas: Assessing The Costs And Consequences Of The 2007–09 Financial Crisis And Its Aftermath, Vol. 8, No. 7; September 2013

King, Rachael; GE Hopes The Industrial Internet Will Mean The End Of Downtime; Wall Street Journal; Http://Blogs.Wsj.Com/

General Electric, Welcome To The Industrial Internet, Http://Www.Geautomation.Com/Industrial-Internet

Guerrera, Francesco; Financial Times: Welch Condemns Share Price Focus; New York; March, 12, 2009; Http://ft.com

Michael E. Porter, Mark R. Kramer; How Companies Can Enrich
Shareholders – And The Planet; Fortune Magazine; August 2015;
Http://Fortune.Com/
Piketty, Thomas; Capital In The Twenty-First Century; Belknap Press;
2014
Solow, Robert; Prospects For Growth: An Interview With Robert
Solow; McKinsey Quarterly; September 2014
Http://Www.Mckinsey.Com
Simonite, Tom; Technology Stalled In 1970; MIT Technology Review;
September 2014; http://Www.Technologyreview.Com/
Surowiecki, James; Companies With Benefits, The New Yorker;
Http://Www.Newyorker.Com/
Unilever, Multinationals, And The B Corp Movement;
Http://Www.Bcorporation.Net

Chapter Three

Auletta, Ken; Blood, Simpler One Woman's Drive To Upend Medical
Testing; The New Yorker; December 2014;
Clynes, Tom Popular Science Magazine: The Boy Who Played With
Fusion:, February 14, 2012; Http://Www.Popsci.Com/
Edwards, Jim; Facebook's Investor Call On The WhatsApp Acquisition;
Business Insider; February 2014,
The Deloitte Millennial Survey Http://Www2.Deloitte.Com/
The Thiel Fellowship; Http://Thielfellowship.Org/About/
USA Today; Change Agents; Http://Www.Usatoday.Com/

Chapter Four

Choose Between Church And Nukes In The Secret Russian Town Of
Sarov; Russia Beyond The Headlines; February 2013;
Http://Rbth.Com/
Drell, Sidney; Hoagland, Jim and Shultz, George; The Man Who Spoke
Truth To Power, Andrei Sakharov's Enduring Relevance; Foreign
Affairs, June 2015

Gorelik, Gennandy; The Riddle Of The Third Idea; Scientific American; August 2011

Khatchadourian, Raffi; A Star In A Bottle - An Audacious Plan To Create A New Energy Source. The New Yorker; March 2014

ITER – The Way To New Energy; Https://Www.Iter.Org/

Mackay, David; Sustainable Energy – Without The Hot Air, UIT; 2008

Sakharov, Andrei, Memoirs; Hutchinson, 1990.

Chapter Five

Betts, Jonathan; Time Restored: The Harrison Timekeepers And R.T. Gould, The Man Who Knew (Almost) Everything;; Oxford University Press; 2011

Bredan, David; A Blog To Watch; Creating The Horological Machine: An Interview With MB&F Founder Max Büsser Part 1 & 2; April 2013; Http://Www.Ablogtowatch.Com/

Doidge, Norman; The Brain That Changes Itself: Stories Of Personal Triumph From The Frontiers Of Brain Science; Penguin; 2008

Estrin, James; Kodak's First Digital Moment; New York Times; August 2015; Http://Nytimes.Com

Luxurious Magazine: MB&F Unveils Stunning Legacy Machine Perpetual Watch Http://Www.Luxuriousmagazine.Com

Mcarthur Christie, Mark; Worn And Wound; The 240 Year Old Pendulum Clock That's More Accurate Than Your Watch; June 2015

Satell, Greg Digital Tonto, The Art Of Shift; April 2015; Http://Www.Digitaltonto.Com/

Shontell, Alyson, Business Insider; Airbnb's First Pitch Deck; March 2015; Http://Uk.Businessinsider.Com/

Sobel, Dava; Longitude – The True Story Of A Lone Genius Who Solved The Greatest Scientific Problem Of His Time; Harper Perennial; 2005

Swift, Jonathan; Gulliver's Travels, Dover Publishers; 1996

Chapter Six

Cadet Harry Hayes, 13, Plants Last Of 888,246 Poppies In Tower Of London Moat; The Telegraph; Http://Www.Telegraph.Co.Uk/

Covey, Stephen R; The 7 Habits Of Highly Effective People;; Simon & Schuster; 1989

How 888,246 Red Ceramic Poppies Captivated Britain And Brought WWI To Life; Quartz; Http://Qz.Com/

Marketing Magazine; Tower Of London 'Poppies' Artist On The Relationship Between Art, Creativity And Life; February 2015; Http://Www.Marketingmagazine.Co.Uk/

Mcphee, Rod; Inside The Ceramic Poppy Factory; The Mirror; August 2014; Http://Www.Mirror.Co.Uk/

WW1 Pottery Poppies Crafted In Derby; The Derby Telegraph; Http://Www.Derbytelegraph.Co.Uk/

Chapter Seven

Chafkin, Max; Udacity's Sebastian Thrun, Godfather Of Free Online Education; Fast Company; November 2013;http://Www.Fastcompany.Com

Fitzgerald, Britney; Steve Jobs' 1983 Speech Makes Uncanny Predictions About The Future; The Huffington Post; March 2012; Http://Www.Huffingtonpost.Com/

Chapter Eight

Fisher, Daniel; Winging It: How Larry Ellison Harnessed Big Data To Win The America's Cup; Forbes Magazine; December 2013; http://Www.Forbes.Com/

Harari, Yuval Noah; Sapiens: A Brief History Of Humankind; Harper 2015,

Harari, Yuval Noah; What Explains The Rise Of Humans?; TED Talk Https://Www.Ted.Com

The America's Cup History https://Www.Americascup.Com/

Swintal, Diane; Tsuchiya, R. Steven; Kamins, Robert; Winging It: ORACLE TEAM USA's Incredible Comeback To Defend The America's Cup; Ragged Mountain Press; 2013

Woo, Stu; Against The Wind;; The Wall Street Journal; http://Www.Wsj.Com/

Chapter Nine

Frazier, Christy L. Martin Fleischmann's Historic Impact; September 2012; http://www.infinite-energy.com/

Huizenga, John R. Cold Fusion: The Scientific Fiasco Of The Century; Oxford University Press; 1994

Mallove, Eugene; Fire From Ice; Searching For The Truth Behind The Cold Fusion Furore;; Infinite Energy; 1999

Chapter Ten

Anderson, Amy; Profiles In Greatness: Wilbur And Orville Wright, To The Wright Brothers, The Word "Impossible" Was Just A Challenge; February, 2010; Http://Www.Success.Com/

Lukasch, Bernd; From Lilienthal To The Wrights; Otto-Lilienthal-Museum; 2003

The Wright Brothers, The Inventors Of The Aerial Age; Smithsonian National Air And Space Museum; Http://Airandspace.Si.Edu/

Final Thoughts

Bosker, Bianca; A Beautiful Mind, Sebastian Thrun Wants To Change The World; Huffington Post; August 2012

Mandela, Nelson; Long Walk To Freedom: The Autobiography Of Nelson Mandela; Abacus; 1995

About the Author

Dean van Leeuwen is the Chief Exploration Officer and a founding partner at TomorrowToday Global, a leader in providing leadership development services to FTSE and Fortune 500 companies. Dean works internationally and frequently lectures and keynotes on the topics of leadership, future trends, strategy and competitive advantage.

He leads the Strategic Insights Laboratory at TomorrowToday Global and is regularly invited to facilitate on executive leadership programmes at top business schools including London Business School and Centre for European Leadership and Development at INSEAD. He is privileged to work across multiple industries for premier organisations including John Lewis Partnership, Nestlé, Novartis, HSBC, Nissan, Topshop, E&Y, Mars Group and Whitbread at both an executive and senior leadership level.

Dean lives in the United Kingdom in a small village near Guildford, London. He is married with a toddler and has a passion for rugby, cycling, wine and partnering with leaders to make a better working world.

If you're interested in contacting Dean, you can email him at dean@tomorrowtodayglobal.com or follow him on Twitter @deanthequester. More information on Dean van Leeuwen can be found on his company website: www.tomorrowtodayglobal.com

About TomorrowToday Global

We live and work in turbulent times of disruptive change. Merely improving on past successes is no longer a guarantee of business success. Your leaders and teams need to understand what is changing - and why - and adapt to new rules for success and failure. This requires shifts in mindset, attitudes, habits and skills.

For the past fourteen years we have been recognised around the world for our ability to anticipate the key trends shaping the world of work. We package our strategic insights in thought-provoking, 'edu-taining' presentations, workshops and leadership programmes that have helped clients across multiple industries to develop and implement strategies that are proving successful in a turbulent and fast changing world.

We were founded in 2001, and have been operating internationally for most of that time. We have offices operating out of United Kingdom, South Africa and Tokyo. We are regularly invited by leading universities, such as Duke Corporate Education, London Business School, European Centre for Executive Development at INSEAD, Henley Management College, Indian School of Business and The Centre for East-West Leadership Studies to partner with them in designing and delivering leadership programmes.

Our facilitators and lecturers consist of highly skilled business and leadership experts, researchers and passionate keynote speakers. All TomorrowToday's delivery team have extensive business experience having worked in leading organisations before joining TomorrowToday Global.

We've worked in over fifty countries, with our business-focused and highly entertaining approach to researching, delivering leadership programmes and presenting insights into the future world of work.

We work hard to help you and your team to see "tomorrow's world today", and to know how you need to think and act differently in the future.

If you want to be part of the new breed of leaders and have recognized that your business needs to change, but you are not sure what this change looks like or how to communicate it, then contact us on quest@tomorrowtodayglobal.com as we'd love to work with you.

Printed in Great Britain
by Amazon.co.uk, Ltd.,
Marston Gate.